SCOTNOTES
Number 23

Neil Munro's

John Splendid

and

The New Road

Ronald W. Renton

Association for Scottish Literary Studies 2007

ACKNOWLEDGMENTS

I would like to thank the following most sincerely for their advice and encouragement while I have been engaged on this project: Professor Douglas Gifford, Lesley Lendrum, Brian D. Osborne, Lorna Smith, James Alison, Charles Munro, the Education Committee of the Association for Scottish Literary Studies and the members of the Neil Munro Society.

Published by
Association for Scottish Literary Studies
Department of Scottish Literature
7 University Gardens
University of Glasgow
Glasgow G12 8QH
www.asls.org.uk

First published 2007

© Ronald W. Renton

A CIP catalogue for this title is available from the British Library

ISBN 978-0-948877-80-3

The Association for Scottish Literary Studies acknowledges the support of the Scottish Arts Council towards the publication of this book

Typeset by AFS Image Setters Ltd, Glasgow
Printed by Bell & Bain Ltd, Glasgow

CONTENTS

	Page
Editors' Foreword	vi
Neil Munro – Life and Work	1
Neil Munro and the Historical Novel	4
John Splendid	6
1. Introduction	6
2. Historical Background	6
3. Structure and Plot Summary	7
4. Themes and Characters	15
5. Setting	21
6. Language and Style	23
7. Local and Literary Influences	26
8. *John Splendid*'s Place in Scottish Highland Literature	29
The New Road	32
1. Introduction	32
2. Historical Background	33
3. Structure and Plot Summary	34
4. Themes and Characters	47
(1) Theme of Murder and Mystery	47
(2) Theme of Disillusionment	48
(3) Theme of Regeneration	53
(4) Theme of the New Road	55
5. Setting	57
6. Language and Style	58
7. Literary Influences	60
8. *The Search*	62
Conclusion	65
Select Bibliography	67
The Works of Neil Munro	69

SCOTNOTES

Study guides to major Scottish writers and literary texts

Produced by the Education Committee
of the Association for Scottish Literary Studies

Series Editors
Lorna Borrowman Smith
Ronald Renton

Editorial Board
Ronald Renton, St Aloysius' College, Glasgow
(Convener, Education Committee, ASLS)
William Aitken, Stevenson College, Edinburgh
Jim Alison, HMI (retired)
Dr Eleanor Bell, University of Strathclyde
Dr Morna Fleming, Beath High School, Cowdenbeath
Professor Douglas Gifford, University of Glasgow
John Hodgart, Garnock Academy, Kilbirnie
Alan Keay, Portobello High School, Edinburgh
Alan MacGillivray, University of Strathclyde
Dr James McGonigal, University of Glasgow
Rev Jan Mathieson, University of Edinburgh
Lorna Ramsay, Fairlie, Ayrshire
Dr Kenneth Simpson, University of Strathclyde
Lorna Borrowman Smith, Stirling

THE ASSOCIATION FOR SCOTTISH LITERARY STUDIES aims to promote the study, teaching and writing of Scottish literature, and to further the study of the languages of Scotland.

To these ends, the ASLS publishes works of Scottish literature; literary criticism and in-depth reviews of Scottish books in *Scottish Studies Review*; short articles, features and news in *ScotLit*; and scholarly studies of language in *Scottish Language*. It also publishes *New Writing Scotland*, an annual anthology of new poetry, drama and short fiction, in Scots, English and Gaelic. ASLS has also prepared a range of teaching materials covering Scottish language and literature for use in schools.

All the above publications are available as a single "package", in return for an annual subscription. Enquiries should be sent to:

ASLS, Department of Scottish Literature, 7 University Gardens, University of Glasgow, Glasgow G12 8QH. Telephone/fax +44 (0)141 330 5309, e-mail **office@asls.org.uk** or visit our website at **www.asls.org.uk**

EDITORS' FOREWORD

The *Scotnotes* booklets are a series of study guides to major Scottish writers and literary texts that are likely to be elements within literature courses. They are aimed at senior pupils in secondary schools and students in further education colleges and colleges of education. Each booklet in the series is written by a person who is not only an authority on the particular writer or text but also experienced in teaching at the relevant levels in schools or colleges. Furthermore, the editorial board, composed of members of the Education Committee of the Association for Scottish Literary Studies, considers the suitability of each booklet for the students in question.

For many years there has been a shortage of readily accessible critical notes for the general student of Scottish literature. *Scotnotes* has grown as a series to meet this need, and provides students with valuable aids to the understanding and appreciation of the key writers and major texts within the Scottish literary tradition.

Lorna Borrowman Smith
Ronald Renton

NOTE ON REFERENCES

The page references in this study guide are to the most recent editions of the novels:
  John Splendid (with introduction by Brian D. Osborne) Black & White Publishing: Edinburgh, 1994
  The New Road (with introduction by Brian D. Osborne) Black & White Publishing: Edinburgh, 1999

Neil Munro – Life and Work

Neil Munro, novelist, journalist and poet, was born in Crombie's Land, Inveraray, Argyll on 3rd June 1863. His mother, Ann Munro, was a kitchen maid, probably in Inveraray Castle. His father has been rumoured to be of the House of Argyll but there is no conclusive evidence for this. Soon after his birth Neil's mother took him to live in his grandmother's house nearby in McVicar's Land and it was in this Gaelic-speaking household that he spent most of his childhood.

He received his formal education at Inveraray Parish School and this he supplemented with his voracious appetite for books. About 1877 he became a clerk to William Douglas, a local lawyer, but found the work tedious. Like so many other young Highlanders, however, he found no other satisfactory employment locally and so on 1st June 1881 he emigrated to Glasgow where he soon began work as a reporter. After a number of posts with different newspapers he joined the *Glasgow Evening News* with which he was to remain happily for almost the rest of his life.

He made his first significant mark on the literary scene in 1896 with *The Lost Pibroch and Other Sheiling Stories*, an innovative collection of short stories which seeks to counteract the sentimentality of "Celtic Twilight" writing and to portray the Highlander accurately and in a language which captures Gaelic idiom. In 1897 he reduced his journalistic work considerably to concentrate on literature, and in 1898 *John Splendid* was published. This, as we will see, is a well-judged historical novel of the seventeenth century dealing with the Montrose-Campbell conflict which culminated in the battle of Inverlochy (1645). In 1899 the partly autobiographical *Gilian the Dreamer* appeared, a study of a young boy whose undisciplined sensitivity impedes his ability to act effectively. This was followed by three more novels: *Doom Castle* (1901), *The Shoes of Fortune* (1901) and *Children of Tempest* (1903), all loosely connected with the aftermath of the Jacobite Rising of 1745.

Munro published many humorous sketches in his unsigned

column "The Looker-On" which appeared every Monday in the *Glasgow Evening News* and, when they later appeared in book form, he adopted for them the pen-name Hugh Foulis. They included stories about the waiter and beadle Erchie MacPherson and the big-hearted commercial traveller Jimmy Swan, but the most celebrated were to be his highly entertaining sketches about the crew of the puffer the *Vital Spark* and their eccentric captain Para Handy. The first of these appeared in 1905 and Munro continued to produce them for most of his working life.

After the novel *Children of Tempest* (1903), Munro turned to fiction which dealt with the contemporary scene with *The Daft Days* (1907) and *Fancy Farm* (1910). In the meantime in 1908 he received the honorary degree of LL.D. from the University of Glasgow and in 1909 he was made a Freeman of Inveraray.

In 1914, returning to the historical novel written in "the Highland manner", he published what many consider to be his finest work, *The New Road*. As we will see, on one level it is a Highland thriller – the hero Aeneas Macmaster's quest for information about his Jacobite father's mysterious death. At a deeper level, however, like Walter Scott's *Waverley* (1814), it examines the condition of the Highlands and the forces which shape change.

The outbreak of the First World War saw Neil Munro's return to full time journalism. In 1915 his elder son Hugh was killed in France, near Aveluy. This trauma, coupled with enormous pressure of work – he became editor of the *Glasgow Evening News* in 1918 – seemed to prevent further large scale literary production. He began another historical novel, *The Search*, intended as a sequel to *The New Road*, but unfortunately it was never completed. He did, however, publish the collection of witty and sophisticated short stories *Jaunty Jock and Other Stories* (1918), and, of course, he continued with his humorous sketches.

In 1927 Munro's health began to fail and he reluctantly retired from the *Evening News* where he was loved and respected. In October 1930 he received a second LL.D., this time from the University of Edinburgh. Two months later he died at his home, "Cromalt", in Helensburgh. In 1931

John Buchan published a collection of his poetry. In 1935 a monument was erected to his memory at the head of Glen Aray near Inveraray. At the dedication ceremony the writer R.B. Cunninghame Graham praised him as "the apostolic successor of Sir Walter Scott".

Munro's literary reputation declined after 1925 when he was accused by Hugh MacDiarmid of writing escapist literature that did not deal with the great national and Highland issues of the day. Modern scholarship, however, shows Munro's critique of Highland – and national – life to be much more acute than MacDiarmid had perceived. His literary reputation is now being restored to its proper place.

Neil Munro and the Historical Novel

Historical novels have been written by some of the world's greatest novelists. In America we have Fenimore Cooper; on the Continent Manzoni, Hugo, Stendhal, Balzac and Tolstoi; in Ireland Edgeworth, in England Dickens, Thackeray and Hardy – and there are, of course, many others who have written historical novels. The person, however, who established the genre and who had a great influence on its development was a Scotsman – Sir Walter Scott. Neil Munro was very familiar with his work.

Before we consider *John Splendid* and *The New Road* it is worth asking ourselves exactly what we understand by a historical novel. It is not enough to describe it simply in such terms as "a story which deals with major events set in the past". The distinguished scholar and critic David Daiches, when discussing the achievement of Sir Walter Scott, discussed the nature of the historical novel in the following terms. A historical novel can be

- essentially an attempt to illustrate those aspects of the life of a previous age which most sharply distinguish it from our own;
- an adventure story, in which the historical elements merely add interest and a sense of importance to the actions described;
- an attempt to use a historical situation to illustrate some aspect of man's fate which has importance and meaning quite apart from the historical situation.[1]

In this hierarchy Daiches considered the first category to be the least important. To attempt to create pictures of a previous period which seek merely to illustrate how different things were in those days from the present is simply to consider the past as picturesque. This is the most superficial and least significant way of treating the past. The third category, on the other hand, he considered to be the most important. Novels which seek to bring the past nearer to us, novels which say something about our human nature and behaviour – these are the best and most worthwhile historical novels.

Scott's best novels come into Daiches' third category. As we study *John Splendid* and *The New Road* it will be useful to consider them in the light of these categories.

John Splendid and *The New Road* evoke the past expertly and vividly. Both could be described as adventure stories in which the historical elements play major parts in the plot. How convincingly, however, do they meet the third category? Do they tell us something important about ourselves and the way we behave as human beings? Do they have something important to say about the human condition and man's fate? Our answer to these questions, once we have studied the novels, will go some way to help us assess the significance of *John Splendid* and *The New Road* as historical novels.

Note
[1] Daiches, David, "Scott's Achievement as a Novelist" in *Literary Essays*, Edinburgh and London: Oliver and Boyd, 1956: p90

John Splendid
The Tale of a Poor Gentleman, and the Little Wars of Lorn (1898)

1. INTRODUCTION

John Splendid can claim to be the first truly Highland novel in Scottish literature. Unlike previous novels dealing with the Highlands by such writers as Scott and Stevenson it is written from the "inside", as it were, by a man who was very familiar with the Gaelic language and Highland history and culture.

Like many of Neil Munro's novels, *John Splendid* takes place in a period of major social change in the Highlands. It deals with the conflict between James Graham, Marquis of Montrose, and the powerful chief of Clan Campbell, the Marquis of Argyll, also known as MacCailein Mòr. This culminates in Montrose's sack of Inveraray in 1644 and subsequent victory over Argyll at Inverlochy in 1645. The novel also examines Highland society under stress, particularly in the persons of the Marquis of Argyll himself (nicknamed Gillesbeg Gruamach or Archibald the Grim) who is anxious to move on from clan warfare to the more peaceful ways of commerce and the rule of law, and his clansman Iain Alainn, John Splendid himself, a swaggering soldier figure who is thirled to the old Highland way of life and whose staunch loyalty compels him to humour his chief and yield to his whims until, finally convinced that his chief is a coward, he rebels.

2. HISTORICAL BACKGROUND

John Splendid is set during the Civil War in Britain which was to culminate in the execution of Charles I in 1649. Although at this period Scotland and England were not united by the Treaty of Union (1707), both countries were riven by internal division between pro-Royalist and anti-Royalist camps. In an endeavour to secure victory for a full-blooded Presbyterian Church in Scotland the latter party drew up and signed the National Covenant in 1638, and later the Solemn League and Covenant in 1643, by which they agreed to assist the English Parliament against Charles on condition that England would, in effect, adopt a Presbyterian Church. These Covenanters were headed by the Marquis of Argyll, probably the most powerful man in the Scotland of his day. The Royalist party was headed by his great rival, James Graham, Marquis of Montrose (who, ironically, had been a leading Covenanter but whose loyalty to his king ultimately transcended all else). *John Splendid* is set during Montrose's military *annus mirabilis* of 1644–45 when he was carrying all before him and seemed unstoppable before his defeat at Philiphaugh. It deals in particular with the sack of Inveraray, the headquarters of the Marquis of Argyll, and the subsequent Battle of Inverlochy.

Although this is the background to the wider political picture, the novel is intensely Highland in its outlook. Montrose's forces relied very heavily on the MacDonalds and their allies. His commander-in-chief was the notorious Alasdair MacDonald, nicknamed Colkitto after his father, and the MacDonalds were the traditional and bitter enemies of Clan Campbell. It is this aspect of clan warfare that becomes all-consuming for most of the protagonists. Munro called his novel a "winter tale" and at one level it is fair to describe the book as a romance since a romantic love strand runs through the story. The political plot, however, which deals with bitter warfare and probes the problems and weaknesses in Highland society gives the story a much harder edge.

3. STRUCTURE AND PLOT SUMMARY

John Splendid moves at a brisk pace and contains a great deal of action. It falls into five sections, each of which is dominated by a fight sequence: the brawl in Inveraray, the battle at the fort on Dunchuach, the battle of Inverlochy (the climax of the story), the confrontation at Dalness and the duel at Tarra Dubh.

Section I: The Return of Elrigmore (Chapters I–VII)

(Throughout the text Munro uses the old spelling *Argile* for the modern *Argyll*; and *M'Iver* for the more usual *MacIver*.)

The first section deals with the homecoming of the narrator of the story, Colin, Young Elrigmore of Glen Shira. His arrival at night in the sleeping Inveraray is vividly described. He has been away fighting for seven years as a soldier of fortune in the Thirty Years War in Germany in the army of Gustavus Adolphus, only to return to find himself in the middle of a civil war at home. We then encounter the character of Gillesbeg Gruamach (Archibald the Grim, the Marquis of Argile) portrayed at this stage as a fierce, unyielding judge. (He was also Scotland's chief law officer.) He is giving judgment on a matter of local politics – the trial of two Catholic MacLachlans, traditional enemies of Clan Campbell from the other side of Loch Finne (the modern Loch Fyne) who also introduce the romantic love theme. John M'Iver of Barbreck, whose nickname is John Splendid, another ex-soldier of fortune, now makes his appearance and Argile, preparing to assemble an army against young Colkitto, offers John Splendid and Elrigmore captaincies. Unlike John Splendid, however, Elrigmore declines the offer as he feels he has too many commitments at home at this stage. His conversation with Betty Brown, his childhood sweetheart and daughter of Provost Brown, is interrupted by Splendid when he asks her to warn her cousin, the young son of the chief of the MacLachlans, that he will be in danger of attack from the MacNicolls who are seeking revenge for the murder of one of their clan by a MacLachlan. There is a fine brawl in the main street of the town but in the end young MacLachlan escapes – back to Betty's house – leaving the seeds of jealousy in Elrigmore's mind that they are lovers.

The story goes on to demonstrate the power of the Kirk and at the same time to show how both Argile and the Kirk have worked to make Inveraray and "real Argile" (present day central Argyllshire), in spite of the odd local quarrel, a very prosperous, modern, and pleasant place in which to live. This is contrasted by an account of the departure of Argile with his army and news of Montrose's victories. It now seems very likely that Betty is being courted by young MacLachlan, and Elrigmore is unsure where he stands with her. In Chapter VII we hear of the shooting of a MacAulay woman who had surprised Elrigmore and his people when they were gathered in the cattle fold. Dying, she foretells disaster for the Campbells and MacCailein Mòr:

"I see the heather above the myrtle on Lhinne-side and MacCailein's head on a post."
(p63)

(Heather is the badge of the MacDonalds, and gall or bog myrtle the badge of the Campbells. The post is an allusion to the spike on the Tolbooth in Edinburgh on which Argile's head was to be impaled after his execution in 1661.)

When she hears that Argile's troops are due home, we are given a tantalising hint that Betty has a more than friendly interest in John Splendid himself. The section ends with the return of the army and the prospect of peace for the winter overcast by the MacAulay prophecy.

In this first section we are introduced to the two main plots of the book: the romantic plot involving Betty, young MacLachlan and the narrator, Elrigmore, and the major plot of the war with Montrose. The supernatural element which will help to provide cohesion for the whole novel is also signalled.

Section II: The Sack of Inveraray (Chapters VIII–XV)

The second part deals with the invasion and sack of Inveraray by Montrose and young Colkitto. The section opens with the freezing winter of 1644 when Loch Finne was frozen and the deer and cattle could cross it. The major plot emerges at once when, at a party in Inveraray Castle, John Splendid sights the lighted beacon on Dunchuach warning of invasion. Elrigmore now honours his word and prepares to join Argile as a soldier. Argile himself, at the sight of his little son, looks for an excuse to take him and his mother out of harm's way. With the encouragement of John Splendid he decides to go to Edinburgh to direct reinforcements to Inveraray. The result is that the Campbells, in the absence of their chief, do not muster to repel the invaders. John Splendid organises the evacuation of the old and the women and children across Loch Finne and all are despatched – with the exception of Betty Brown and the *oe* (grandchild) of Peggy Mhor whom she was trying to save. When the enemy attack, John Splendid, Elrigmore and Sir Donald are obliged to retreat to the glen of Eas-a-Chosain behind the town. Elrigmore has been wounded, so they stay in a cave there until their presence is spotted. They then make their way in the dark to the fort on the top of Dunchuach, having been joined by young MacLachlan who is seeking Betty Brown and the child.

Once in the fort there is a stirring battle as they are attacked by Montrose's forces, first on one side and then on the other. They are warned of the second attack by the heroic action of the Protestant minister, Gordon, who joins them at this point. Further proof of his sterling character is given when he insists on leaving the fort to go out and obtain water for his fellow soldiers. On his way back he stops to give a drink to a dying enemy, a Glencoe MacDonald, but is knocked unconscious by other enemy clansmen. When he comes to, however, he informs the others that the MacDonald had told him:

> "There's a woman and child in the wood of Strongara." (p109)

John Splendid and Elrigmore set out to look for Betty and the child but they cannot locate them in the dark.

Next day they find them. In the course of conversation Betty hints to Elrigmore that John Splendid is the child's father. Elrigmore tries to be gallant towards her but she gives him no encouragement. On hearing that Montrose's men are leaving the town they seek to move to a safer position but have to take refuge in a barn near the road.

The soldiers pass and then, as Montrose himself passes on his own, the baby cries. Montrose clearly hears but moves on, doing nothing to harm them.

After the departure of Montrose, Argile returns to his ruined town. He is ashamed of himself for having deserted his people. He blames John Splendid for being "a devil's counsellor" (p142) and giving him false advice.

This section contrasts the cowardice and weakness of the Marquis and his plausible yet well-intentioned Highland adviser, John Splendid, with the nobility of action of the Lowland minister Gordon and the Lowland general Montrose.

Section III: Campbell v Montrose at the Battle of Inverlochy (1645) (Chapters XVI–XX)

Section three opens with John Splendid telling Elrigmore that he did not deny paternity of the child in Betty's care, partly out of good manners and partly because, by comparison with himself, Elrigmore will shine in the lady's eyes. Argile leads his army off to avenge the humiliation of the sack of Inveraray and Dame Dubh, a crazed old woman, appears for the first time at the head of Glen Aray and follows them. They cross a frozen Loch Awe to the first night's camp in Glen Noe where John Splendid recites the ballad "Sergeant of Pikes". Argile fraternises with his soldiers and there is no sign of hesitancy or cowardice in his behaviour.

As they move north the Campbell looting of enemy Stewart territory is fierce in reprisal for their previous suffering, in spite of Argile's orders to the contrary. As they leave to cross Loch Leven they hear of Dame Dubh's prophecy which has the same import as the MacAulay woman's. Argile sets up camp at Inverlochy and then sends out John Splendid and Elrigmore to discover the whereabouts of Montrose. After taking rest in a cottage at the foot of Loch Oich they meet the bard Iain Lom MacDonald. A dispute breaks out between them when Iain Lom taunts them with MacCailein's cowardly departure from Inveraray. Suddenly all three are taken prisoner by some MacGregors and are brought to Montrose. Iain Lom is identified as the Bard of Keppoch and he reports the location of Argile's force. Montrose puts John Splendid and Elrigmore on parole. Montrose then decides to surprise Argile's army with a countermarch to the south via Glen Tarf, Corryarick and Glen Nevis in appalling winter conditions. The scouts have, of course, failed in their mission. As prisoners of war they are not allowed to join in the battle but they see it from a hill in Brae Lochaber. The Campbells are soundly defeated (although details are not revealed until later) and the scouts see six fugitives heading in their direction pursued by Ogilvy's cavalry. One of these is Gordon, the minister.

Section three is the climax of the novel, the countermarch of Montrose's MacDonalds and Athole Stewarts, building up to their triumph at Inverlochy. From now on the action of the book deals with the retreat to Inveraray of John Splendid, Elrigmore and Argile himself.

Section IV: Retreat through Glencoe and Rannoch Moor (Chapters XXI–XXVIII)

Section four deals with the flight of the refugees whom John Splendid and Elrigmore join as they head south. Gordon scolds John Splendid for not having given Argile sound advice and eventually discloses that Argile left in a galley before the commencement of battle. Dame Dubh reappears and reviles the retreating supporters of Argile. They reach Glencoe and receive hospitality in a blind woman's cottage. It becomes apparent that her husband had recently died of plague – a situation which terrifies John Splendid and the other Highlanders. Gordon, however, copes very well, kissing the woman's hand on departure.

They then make for Glen Etive. When they reach the big house in Dalness they find the fires lit and food on the table. They are too hungry and fatigued to resist and they settle down for the night. Elrigmore and Gordon have a conversation about Argile in which Gordon explains that the reason for the Marquis's weak behaviour is that he has been flattered into not knowing his duty by people like John Splendid and Auchinbreac, and the consequence was his "shabby flight" from Inverlochy. John Splendid overhears this and assaults Gordon. Then Dame Dubh arrives battering at the door with news that the apparently hospitable house is a trap and that the Glencoe MacDonalds will soon be upon them. They leave and seal off all the exits except the front door with the idea of locking the enemy inside once they have entered. However, this plan fails and they have to separate and make their own ways south intending to rendezvous at the Bridge of Urchy (modern spelling: Orchy). Elrigmore finally finds shelter in the inn at Tynree (King's House) where a bogus spae-wife informs him that MacLachlan is making progress in his wooing of Betty. He then gets lost on Rannoch Moor but finally meets up with John Splendid just before the mist rises. They then proceed to the Bridge of Urchy, but the others have already gone, so they proceed homewards.

In section four, in addition to the vivid descriptions of the flight of the fugitives through dreadful weather in Glencoe, we learn of the essential weakness in John Splendid's character which Gordon clearly identifies – that he is unable to make tough decisions when advising or dealing with friends like Argile or the blind widow in Glencoe, although he can be hard on his enemies easily enough:

"Did I not say you knew your duty in hate better than in affection?" (p218)

Furthermore, the appearance of Dame Dubh at Dalness assists the cohesion of the story, although her apparent recovery from her previous crazed state is less satisfactorily explained.

Section V: Return to Inveraray and Resolution (Chapters XXIX–XXXV)
Section five opens with the two soldiers' return to Inveraray where the houses are being rebuilt, "for MacCailein's first thought on his return from Edinburgh had been the comfort of the common people" (p277). They go to the castle to report to their chief. When they meet him he confesses his shame for his behaviour at Inverlochy but blames his

flattering advisers for their part, saying that the only person whose advice he could trust was the blunt Lowland minister, Gordon. Eventually he pushes John Splendid for his true opinion on his behaviour at Inverlochy. John can dissemble no longer, and, in spite of clan loyalties, he finally speaks his mind, saying that his chief has gone soft, putting books before valour. He then throws down his dagger in a challenge. When they leave, Argile weeps. To counterbalance this impression of a weak and indecisive character, the narrator then momentarily "fast-forwards" us to the death of Argile when he was executed in 1661 to show us that it was indeed noble. (The main plot ends at this point and the remaining chapters (XXXI–XXXV) deal with the resolution of the romantic plot.)

Elrigmore meets Betty who is walking with John Splendid. She tackles him again on the paternity of the baby grandchild of Peggy Mhor. By not denying it he appears to plead guilty (although we know he is not), probably to enhance Elrigmore in the lady's esteem. On hearing that MacLachlan has been bragging openly in the town of a love affair with Betty, Elrigmore becomes incensed for the lady's honour and he and John Splendid contrive that he should challenge MacLachlan to a duel. This takes place at Tarra Dubh and MacLachlan is wounded. A skilly woman is sent for who turns out to be none other than Dame Dubh. She is able to reveal that MacLachlan is the father of Peggy Mhor's grandchild and that he appeared to be courting Betty only to have access to the baby. He is not in love with her. MacLachlan marries Nannie Ruadh, who happily takes the child as her own, and Elrigmore and Betty develop a loving relationship and will eventually marry. After his dispute with Argile, John Splendid has resolved to take up his old trade as soldier of fortune and sets off for foreign climes. Only in the very last lines does it become clear to Betty that he is not the father of the child, and, as he departs, she stares after him realising too late that she has lost the man she really loves.

In the fifth section the political plot is resolved with

MacCailein's admission of guilt and his accusation of his false advisers. He was, however, a man "tossed between philosophies" (p285) and the conflict of his allegiance to traditional Highland values with his vision of a more modern "civilised" future points towards the Highland resistance to change which will have to be faced up to. The love plot is conveniently resolved by the revelations of Dame Dubh. (Unfortunately, although she is a useful linking device in the story, the complete alteration in her character from crazed sybil to sympathetic nurse and her unlikely appearances at convenient times mean that the demands of the plot have resulted in a measure of inconsistency in her characterisation. There is, however, historical evidence for the existence of a crazed sybil who followed the Campbell army.)[1] The final twist, when Betty realises that she has lost John Splendid, ensures that the novel does not have a conventional romantic ending.

4. THEMES AND CHARACTERS

Neil Munro has been accused of not dealing with the problems of the Gael in his own time and *John Splendid* is obviously a historical novel which deals principally with the age old Campbell-MacDonald conflict, but at another level it is exploring deeper themes which are of more modern concern. It probes the weakness of aspects of Highland society and also explores the need for, and process of, change in the Highlands – a theme which he will return to in *The New Road* (1914) and which is still a matter of concern today. These themes become apparent in a study of the main characters.

Colin, Young Elrigmore, the Highland narrator of the novel, is in his late twenties and is an experienced soldier. He had studied at Glasgow University and then gone, like John Splendid, to fight as a mercenary in the European wars. He is a kind, civilised, serious-minded man: John Splendid nicknames him "Sobersides" (p254). In spite of his worldly experience fighting abroad he is still modest and shy ("blate" (p294) his future father-in-law calls him), and, although he is in love with Betty from the very beginning, it takes to the very end of the book for him to make his feelings known to her.

Like many of Sir Walter Scott's major characters, Elrigmore takes the reasonable, middle ground between extremes. He has the traditional virtues of loyalty to his clan chief and fights in defence of his own lands but expresses shame at the savagery of the revenge the Campbells take after the sack of Inveraray. He also occupies the middle ground between John Splendid and Argile. He enjoys the friendship of John Splendid but has none of his boastfulness, flattery or contempt for progress. On the other hand, although he is loyal to Argile and as an educated man understands his desire for progress, he knows his duty in the face of his chief's cowardice at Inverlochy. He makes sure by accompanying John Splendid when they visit him on their return that there will be no flattery this time and Argile will hear the plain truth about his actions.

Elrigmore is also of interest from a technical point of view. He is the narrator of the story and, given the honesty of his character, we feel that his account of events is a fair one. Furthermore, he narrates the story from the comfort of his old age and we find the narrative broken frequently with melancholy retrospects. These give the impression that, although Elrigmore regrets the passing of his earlier life, he is nonetheless viewing the world from a happier and more civilised time and that the world has in fact moved on from the bloodletting of 1645.

John Splendid (John M'Iver of Barbreck), the "poor gentleman" of the book's sub-title, is a veteran of the Thirty Years War. He is in his forties, is vain in his dress and is moderately good-looking. He is extremely boastful, in the mould of Stevenson's Alan Breck, although not as strongly drawn as his counterpart in *Kidnapped*. He comes nearest to him in the episode when he and Elrigmore are lost in the Moor of Rannoch and they kill two hounds which their pursuers have set on them:

> "Oh, I'm the most wonderful fellow ever stepped heather, and I could be making a song on myself there and then if occasion allowed." (p266)

(Compare Alan Breck's boastfulness in *Kidnapped* after the fight in the roundhouse where he exclaims "Am I no a bonnie fechter?" and composes a song praising his own prowess as a swordsman: "This is the song of the sword of Alan".)[2] Yet in spite of being a braggart John Splendid is very popular with all around, male and female.

Above all he is a good, brave (sometimes superstitious) soldier in whom Argyll has the utmost confidence and there is no doubt that he is well-practised and practical in the skills of war. Furthermore, although he may have been a mercenary selling his services to the highest bidder abroad, at home his loyalty to his clan and chief are without question. And herein lies his weakness: such is his desire not to offend he will not give blunt advice and speak his mind forcefully to his friends and to his chief for fear of hurting them and in some way diminishing their self-esteem. Consequently, when he sees that Argile, terrified as Montrose prepares to attack Inveraray, is intent upon deserting his people and fleeing to Edinburgh on the pretext of directing reinforcements to his town, he flatters his chief by telling him he must go because:

> "There's not a man out there but would botch the whole business if you sent him ... it must be his lordship or nobody." (p76)

and later he says:

> "He'll know himself his going looks bad without my telling him, and I would at least leave him the notion that we were blind to his weakness." (p78)

At the end of the book, after Argile has allowed himself to be seriously misdirected by Auchinbreac to forsake the field at Inverlochy, he pushes John Splendid very hard to know his opinion of his action. Only then, reluctantly, in anger and disdain, does he finally give his true opinion to his chief – an opinion that will forbid any chance of future reconciliation:

> "Purgatory's your portion, Argile, for a Sunday's work that makes our name a mock to-day across the envious world ... but here's my dagger ... it's the last tool I'll handle in the service of a scholar. Tomorrow the old big wars [abroad] for me." (p283)

It is the weakness of over-politeness, the desire not to offend when his duty is otherwise, that Munro singles out here as the crucial weakness in the Highland character. As Argile says of John Splendid:

> "You and your kind are the weak, strong men of our Highland race. The soft tongue and the dour heart; the good man at most things but at your word." (p142)

John Splendid also illustrates the other problem of the Highlands which Munro seems to be hinting at – the reluctance to accept change. He accuses Argile of being too much of a scholar, of living in a world of books and documents:

> "Paper and ink will be the Gael's undoing; my mother taught me, and my mother knew. So long as we lived by our hands we were the world's invincibles." (p284)

He cannot see that the Gael must move with the times and prefers to believe, like his namesake Fergus MacIvor in Sir Walter Scott's *Waverley*, in the old heroic values.

Gillesbeg Gruamach (Archibald the Grim), the Marquis of Argile, (also known as **MacCailein Mòr**, the traditional name of the Campbell chief) illustrates these problems from the other side. He is the most complex character in the book and is portrayed as something of a Jekyll and Hyde figure, the tyrannical and bigoted judge of chapter II supporting clan faction and at the same time the sensitive scholarly man who seeks peace, progress and prosperity for his people:

> ... the place was swamped by incomers ... all brought up here by Gillesbeg Gruamach Marquis of Argile, to teach his clans the arts of peace and merchandise. (p11)

He has "come – or wellnigh – come to the conclusion that this life was never designed by the Creator to be spent in the turmoil of faction and field" (p139). He is caught between the values of the clan system and the values and ideas of the more modern world into which he is trying to bring his clan. Endeavouring to rationalise his position he is indecisive and because he is not strongly and honestly advised by John Splendid and Auchinbreac he fails in his duty to his people with terrible consequences at the two most crucial junctures of the book: the sack of Inveraray and the battle of Inverlochy. Not surprisingly does he berate John Splendid for his flattery and his easy words:

> "One word of honest duty from you at that time had kept me in Inneraora though Abijah's array and Jeroboam's horse and foot were coming down the glens." (p141)

Nonetheless, Argile has the vision and the will to introduce a more modern and peaceful way of life to his people and his reputation is saved by Elrigmore's forecast of his honourable death seventeen years later (p286).

These Highlanders with their faults of dishonest kindness and indecisiveness are set against the blunt Presbyterian minister, Gordon, and the man of action, Montrose – both, significantly, Lowlanders.

Master Gordon shows fearless courage all through the novel, from his arrival in the fort of Dunchuach where he tends to a dying enemy at peril of his own life to his flight through Glencoe where he kisses the hand of the blind woman who may well have the plague. He is the loyal and uncompromisingly truthful chaplain of Argile, and he identifies the cause of the latter's faults as the advisers who keep "from him every rumour that might vex his ear" and colour "every event in such a manner as will please him" (p240) to the extent that they were responsible for his dereliction of duty at Inverlochy and his "shabby flight" (p243). He is unyielding in his criticism of John Splendid as one who "knew your duty in hate better than in affection" (p218).

James Graham, Marquis of Montrose, likewise, is contrasted with the two Highlanders as a man who is decisive and the soul of honour. Examples of this are in his quite deliberate connivance at the presence of the fugitives in Glen Aray when he hears the child cry, and his extremely honourable treatment of John Splendid and Elrigmore as prisoners of war on the countermarch and at the field of Inverlochy. Indeed, he shows a magnanimity to them which transcends internal political factions because of their honourable achievements as Scottish soldiers in the European wars:

> "as Cavaliers who, clansmen or no clansmen of the Campbell chief, have done well for old Scotland's name abroad, I think you deserve a little more consideration at our hands at this juncture than common prisoners of war can lay claim to." (p184)

Finally, a few words require to be said about **Betty Brown** and **the ending of the novel**. Although Betty has a relatively small part in the action she is a strong character. She strives to have young MacLachlan protected from being assaulted by the MacNicolls in Chapter 4. When Inveraray is laid waste by Montrose she takes to the hills with the abandoned grandchild of Peggy Mhor whom she bravely protects. They are eventually found by Elrigmore and John Splendid. At this point it becomes clear that she is greatly attracted to John Splendid himself, but matters go no further because she believes that he is the father of the abandoned child and is very angry that he will not acknowledge this. Near the end she challenges him again on this matter. He does not deny it, probably sacrificing his own chances with her to enhance Elrigmore in her esteem. Only on the very last page does she finally realise that he is not the father of the child (p334). Through misunderstanding she has lost the man she really loves. (And there is the strong possibility that Elrigmore will realise this too!) This subtle twist means that *John Splendid* does not have a conventional romantic ending. Betty will marry Elrigmore – but will probably always be haunted by the dream of the man she really wanted.

5. SETTING

Like almost all of Munro's fiction, *John Splendid* is very much a novel of place. It is set principally in the Argyllshire town of Inveraray and its environs (although, anachronistically, Munro describes the modern town built in the 18th century rather than the 17th century village) and follows the journey of John Splendid and Elrigmore north through Glen Noe and Loch Leven, as far as Kilcumin (Fort Augustus) in Inverness-shire, and south again via Corryarrick, Glen Nevis and Inverlochy (where battle is joined), Glencoe and Glen Orchy. (See map at the beginning of the novel.) The accuracy and care devoted to the portrayal of landscape is such that it becomes a major character in the book, especially in those scenes describing Montrose's counter-march south from Kilcumin via Corryarrick, Glen Roy and Glen Nevis (Chapter XIX) and the flight of the fugitives in Glencoe (Chapter XXIV).

In Chapter XIX the plight of Montrose's men marching through the mountains of a freezing winter is graphically described as they make their way south in appalling conditions in order to surprise the army of the Campbells at Inverlochy:

> The pass of Corryarick met us with a girning face and white fangs. On Tarf-side there was a rough bridle-path that the wind swept the snow from, and our progress was fairly easy. Here the drifts lay waist high, the horses plunged to the belly-bands, the footmen pushed through in a sweat. It was like some Hyperborean hell, and we the doomed wretches sentenced to our eternity of toil. We had to climb up the shoulder of the hill, now

> among tremendous rocks, now through water unfrozen, now upon wind-swept ice, but the snow – the snow – the heartless snow was our constant companion. It stood in walls before, it lay in ramparts round us, it wearied the eye to a most numbing pain. Unlucky were they who wore trews, for the same clung damply to knee and haunch and froze, while the stinging sleet might flay the naked limb till the blood rose among the felt of the kilted, but the suppleness of the joints was unmarred. (p173)

In Chapter XXIV Elrigmore and John Splendid with the five other fugitives are in flight after the Campbell defeat at Inverlochy. They seek their way through the enemy territory of Glencoe again impeded by atrocious weather as they try to make their way home to Inveraray:

> But if we rejoiced in the rains of Bavaria, there was no cause for glee in those torrents of Glencoe, for they made our passage through the country more difficult and more dangerous than it was before. The snow on the ground was for hours a slushy compost, that the foot slipped on at every step, or that filled the brogue with a paste that nipped like brine. And when the melting snow ran to lower levels the soil itself, relaxing the rigour of its frost, became as soft as butter and as unstable to the foot. The burns filled to the lip and brawled over, new waters sprung up among the rocks and ran across our path, so that we were for ever wading and slipping and splashing and stumbling on a route that seemed never to come to any end or betterment. (p220)

and

> It was with almost a jocund heart I turned my back on Glencoe as we took a drove-path up from the river. But I glanced with a shiver down its terrible distance upon that nightmare of gulf and eminence, of gash, and peaks afloat upon swirling mists. It lay, a looming

terror, forgotten of heaven and unfriendly to man (as one might readily imagine), haunted for ever with wailing airs and rumours, ghosts calling in the deeps of dusk and melancholy, legends of horrors and remorse. (p223)

6. LANGUAGE AND STYLE

In a letter of 1894 to his future publisher William Blackwood, Neil Munro shows that he is well aware of the limitations of sentimental writing, often described as the Kailyard, which was very popular at that time. He clearly has no intention of imitating that approach. In this letter he also complains that "all the men who have dealt with the romance of the Highlands hitherto have been Lowlanders, writing from the outside" and have no real feel for their subject: and that, of course, includes Scott and Stevenson.

It is with all this in mind that Munro, a fluent Gaelic speaker familiar with Gaelic literature and tradition, seeks to give a more genuine, unsentimental account of the Highlands and the Highlander in his first ground-breaking collection of short stories called *The Lost Pibroch and Other Sheiling Stories* which Blackwood was to publish for him in 1896.

In this collection a major feature in his attempt to represent the Gael more accurately is his experimental use of language. In the past writers, even Sir Walter Scott and James Hogg, had represented the Gael's tongue in their writing in a way that was at best inaccurate and at worst parodic and condescending. Munro would have none of this. Instead he moved to a much more authentic Gaelic-English which above all involves the frequent employment of Gaelic syntax. We can see Munro doing this in the story "Black Murdo" from *The Lost Pibroch* collection in this phrase:

"it's lame he'll be all his days anyway."

This goes neatly into Gaelic as

"*sann crubach a bhios e fad a laithean codhiu.*"

In addition he incorporates Gaelic idioms here and there.

For example, for "twilight" he uses the expression "the mouth of the night" which is a literal translation of the Gaelic phrase *beul na h-oidhche*. Throughout the stories there is also a gentle spattering of Gaelic words, for example *iolair* (eagle) and *caman* (shinty stick), but not enough to hold up the English reader's progress. He also includes many Gaelic place-names and further enriches the Gaelic atmosphere by including Gaelic proverbs and the names of pipe tunes. Furthermore, and a point not often noted, Munro also includes a remarkably wide range of Scots words and idioms – which would, of course, have infiltrated the Highland speech of Inveraray and its environs long before standard English.

The effect of all this is to create the illusion for the reader that he/she is initiated into the language and culture of Munro's Highland characters in much the same way that Lewis Grassic Gibbon's *Speak of the Mearns* takes us into the world of his east coast region of Scotland. Munro, however, has the more difficult task to accomplish. He has a completely different language to represent as opposed to a dialect of Scots.

In *John Splendid* (and later in *The New Road*) this approach is continued but it is used more sparingly and is handled with more confidence and control than in the earlier stories. Indeed, the author enjoys a sly joke now and again with such phrases as:

> "What is it ye want?" he asked MacNicoll, burring out his Gaelic *r*'s with punctilio."
> (p39)

There are, of course, no "r's" in the above quotation, so we must assume that the character spoke the Gaelic words "*Dè tha sibh ag iarraidh?*" – "What do you want?"

Authenticity of Highland atmosphere is also gained by incorporating genuine Gaelic proverbs such as:

> "*Ruigidh an ro-ghiullach[d] air an ro-ghalar*" –
> "Good nursing will overcome the worst disease." (p86)[3]

and

"*Am fear a bhios fad aig an aiseig, gheibh e thairis uaireigin*" – "The man who waits long at the ferry will get over some day." (p211)[4]

And a nice Gaelic touch is obtained when he has John Splendid refer to his gun as *Mairi Og (Young Mary)* (p101) just as the famous bard Duncan Ban MacIntyre referred to his gun as *NicCoiseim (Coiseam's daughter)*.[5]

Again as in *The Lost Pibroch* collection Munro incorporates many Scots words and idioms such as: *gleg* (quick), *mowdie* (mole), *pay the lawing* (pay the tavern bill), *hamesucken* (the crime of assaulting someone in their own home), *crouse* (proud), *tirling at the pin* (knocking at the door). These are very appropriate for they would be the language of the Lowland burghers whom Gillesbeg Gruamach had encouraged to settle in Argyll to "teach his clan the arts of peace and merchandise".

The many fine and detailed descriptions of nature in this novel have often been praised for their vividness and sharpness of focus. These passages also give this book its greatest Gaelic authenticity, for in them nature is described minutely down to different plants, grasses and animals in a specific location to give sensuous delight in the manner of the great eighteenth century nature bards Duncan Ban MacIntyre and Alexander MacDonald. The following passage will serve to illustrate:

> "I know corries in Argile that whisper silken to the winds with juicy grasses, corries where the deer love to prance deep in the cool dew, and the beasts of far-off woods come in bands at their seasons and together rejoice. I have seen the hunter in them and the shepherd too, coarse men in life and occupation, come sudden among the blowing rush and whispering reed, among the bog-flower and the cannoch, unheeding the moor-hen and the cailzie-cock rising, or the stag of ten at pause, while they stood, passionate adventurers in a rapture of the mind, held as it were by the spirit of such places as they lay in a sloeberry bloom of haze, the spirit of old good songs,

the baffling surmise of the piper and the bard. To those corries of my native place will be coming in the yellow moon of brock and foumart – the beasts that dote on the autumn eves – the People of Quietness [fairies]; have I not seen their lanthorns and heard their laughter in the night? – so that they must be blessed corries, so endowed since the days when the gods dwelt in them without tartan and spear in the years of the peace that had no beginning." (pp223–224)

Of this passage John Buchan observes,

> [Neil Munro's] prose seems to me more strictly poetic than his verse. It is true prose in structure, but it trembles often on the edge of song.[6]

7. LOCAL AND LITERARY INFLUENCES

As a boy there was much to inspire Neil Munro's interest on the subject of the sack of the Marquis of Argyll's Inveraray by the army of Montrose in 1644. It was part of local folk tradition, and many stories concerning it were recorded by the great folk collector John Francis Campbell with whose work Munro had certainly come in contact. Another incident which might well have served to foster his interest took place October 1877, when he was fourteen years old and beginning work in a lawyer's office. There was, as Blanche Dugdale tells us, a huge fire in Inveraray castle:

> ... nothing of irreplaceable value was lost, except the only authentic portrait of the "Great Marquis" of Argyll, which had hung in the hall. It had only recently been brought there from another room, to match the picture of the Marquis of Montrose, just acquired by my Uncle Lorne.
> There was an old woman in Inveraray town who had shaken her head and predicted calamity when she heard that Montrose's picture had been brought to the Castle. Two

hundred years had not obliterated the memory of the winter when he and his wild Irish carried fire and sword into the heart of Real Argyll. But her warnings were unheeded by the Victorian generation. For a few days, or weeks, the portraits of the two Marquises hung side by side. The lightning from Heaven put an end to the unnatural companionship of these two mortal enemies.[7]

With his keen interest in local history and his instinct for a good story this incident would have made a big impression on the young Munro and no doubt inspired him to learn more about the subjects of the portraits.

Sir Walter Scott's *A Legend of Montrose*

The major literary source on which Munro draws is Sir Walter Scott's *A Legend of Montrose* (1819). In this novel we meet the character who was probably the inspiration for the eponymous John Splendid. He is Captain Dugald Dalgetty, a selfish, garrulous and rather pedantic mercenary who has fought like John Splendid in the Thirty Years War in Germany for Gustavus Adolphus. However, back in Scotland he is still prepared to sell his services to the highest bidder – an action which would have been inconceivable to John Splendid. The similarity with *A Legend of Montrose* does not, however, end there. The narrator of the book, Young Elrigmore, is also a Scottish mercenary, both novels have a large part of their setting in Inveraray and both deal very specifically with the Battle of Inverlochy (1645). In that battle the Royalist forces of Montrose and his general, Alasdair MacDonald (Colkitto, although this was more commonly his father's nickname), defeat the Marquis of Argyll, the leader of the Covenanting forces (who was, like Montrose, later to meet his fate at the Grassmarket in 1661 and have his head impaled on the same spike on Edinburgh's Tolbooth). Furthermore, references to Sir James Turner's *Pallas Armata*, a handbook on the art of war, to "The Children of the Mist" (although Munro makes these MacAulays rather than MacGregors), to bloodhounds in pursuit of a hero and to supernatural predictions all appear in Scott as well as in Munro. The novels are, however, told from opposing points of view, Munro's from the Campbell perspective and Scott's from the Royalist perspective. More significantly, unlike its literary ancestor, *John Splendid* only once touches upon the full national significance of the war: when Auchinbreac, Argyll's adviser, persuades him not to lead his men at Inverlochy because

> "you are the mainstay of a great **national** movement, depending for its success on your life, freedom and continued exertion." (p243)

Iain Lom MacDonald's *Là Inbhir Lochaidh* (The Day of Inverlochy)

Although Munro clearly used Scott as a source there is one significant respect in which he differs. Scott follows the tradition that just before the battle of Inverlochy MacIlduy (Cameron) transmitted the news of the whereabouts of Argyll's army to Montrose. Munro follows the tradition that it was Iain (John) Lom MacDonald, the great 17th century Gaelic bard, who brought this news. He was certainly familiar with his greatest song, *Là Inbhir Lochaidh* ("The Day of Inverlochy") which describes Montrose's victory triumphantly and vividly, and, indeed, Munro puts the following into Iain Lom's mouth in Chapter XX:

> "There are plenty to fight; there's but one to make the song of the fight [i.e. *Là Inbhir Lochaidh*], and that's John MacDonald with your honours' leave." (p184)

The idea that John Splendid and Elrigmore as prisoners of war watched the battle from a hill in Brae Lochaber probably owes its origin to Iain Lom's declaration in the poem that he watched the battle from a hill above Inverlochy:

> *Dhìrich mi moch madainn Dòmnaich*
> *Gu braigh caisteal Inbhir Lòchaidh;*
> *Chunnaic mi 'n t-arm dol an òrdugh,*
> *'S bha buaidh a' bhlàir le Clann Dòmhnaill.*[8]

(Early on Sunday morning I climbed the brae above the Castle of Inverlochy. I saw the army arraying for battle, and victory on the field was with Clan Donald.)

The song goes on to describe in gory detail the slaughter of the Campbell army. Among the Campbell casualties was Auchinbreac, Gillesbeg Gruamach's general.

Robert Louis's Stevenson's *Kidnapped*

Neil Munro openly admired the work of Robert Louis Stevenson, and his novel *Kidnapped* (1886) has clearly influenced *John Splendid*. Both are very much novels of place and contain vivid descriptions of the Scottish Highlands with the main characters of both stories getting lost on the wild and lonely Rannoch Moor. Both novels involve a journey, and the pairing of the two main characters Alan Breck and David Balfour in *Kidnapped* is replicated by Munro with his John Splendid and Colin, Young Elrigmore. There are, however, significant differences. Instead of the two men coming from either side of the Highland/Lowland divide, Munro's characters are both Highland but followers of Clan Campbell and, therefore, opposed to the Royalist/Stuart cause, and Elrigmore, instead of being a callow youth like David Balfour, is in his late twenties and already a veteran of European wars. John Splendid, on the other hand, shares much of the boastfulness and swagger of Stevenson's Alan Breck.

8. *JOHN SPLENDID*'S PLACE IN SCOTTISH HIGHLAND LITERATURE

John Splendid is the first novel about the Highlands of Scotland written by a Highlander "from the inside". There was no tradition of novel writing in Gaelic for Munro to draw on – the first Gaelic novel, *Dun-Aluinn* by Iain MacCormaic, was not written until 1912[9] and, when it did come, was not to be compared with Munro's own efforts –

so he was very much a pioneer and on the whole a very successful one. If we omit the rather strained and inconsistent device of Dame Dubh as a supernatural means of linking the story and perhaps also the convolutions of the romantic plot towards the end, we have a very powerfully executed story about a major event in Highland history. Hugh MacDiarmid's criticism that Munro was parochial and that he preferred "the little wars of Lorn to the conflict of real life"[10] is unfair. Munro was seeking to write a specifically Highland novel and, though the wars of Lorn may have seemed little enough to MacDiarmid on a British or world canvas, to the Highlander they were all too real. Furthermore, Munro, in his analysis of Highland society and the process of change and modernisation in the Highlands, is opening up an investigation which is already hinted at in his short story "The Lost Pibroch" and which would continue to interest him throughout the rest of his literary career. It would also interest such contemporaries of MacDiarmid's as Neil Gunn, Naomi Mitchison, Fionn MacColla and Compton MacKenzie in the Scottish Literary Renaissance of the 1930s and 1940s.

Notes
[1] Williams, Ronald, *The Heather and the Gale*, Colonsay: House of Lochar, 1997: p125
[2] Stevenson, R.L., *Kidnapped and Catriona*, Letley, Emma (Ed.), Oxford: Oxford University Press, 1986: Ch10, p62
[3] Nicolson, Alexander, *A Collection of Gaelic Proverbs and Familiar Phrases*, Edinburgh, 1881: p341
[4] Ibid. p11
[5] "Oran do'n Ghunna dh'an ainm NicCoiseim" (No. 27), *The Songs of Duncan Ban MacIntyre*, MacLeod, Angus (Ed.), Edinburgh: Oliver and Boyd, 1952: pp226–229
[6] *The Poetry of Neil Munro*, Buchan, John (Ed.), Edinburgh: William Blackwood, 1931: pp8–9
[7] Dugdale, Blanche (daughter of Marquis of Lorne's sister), *Family Homespun*, London, 1940: pp6–7
[8] *Orain Iain Luim*, lines 190–194, MacKenzie, Annie (Ed.), Edinburgh: Scottish Academic Press, 1964: p20
[9] MacCormaic, Iain, *Dun-Aluinn*, Glasgow: Alasdair MacLabhruinn, 1912

[10] MacDiarmid, Hugh, "Neil Munro", *The Scottish Educational Journal*, 3rd July, 1925 (Collected in MacDiarmid, Hugh, *Contemporary Scottish Studies*, Riach, Alan (Ed.), Manchester: Carcanet, 1995: pp18–23)

The New Road (1914)

1. INTRODUCTION

The New Road was published in 1914. In it Munro returns to the literary vein which had been so successful for him in the early 1900s, the world of historical romance, after trying his hand at two contemporary novels *The Daft Days* (1907) and *Fancy Farm* (1910).

This novel is an accomplished and entertaining Jacobite romance set around 1733. (Conflicting internal evidence makes the dates 1732 and 1734 also possibilities.)[1] The setting is Inveraray, Inverness and all the countryside between as the two protagonists, the inexperienced Aeneas Macmaster and his veteran mentor Ninian Macgregor Campbell travel from Argyll to the country of Simon Fraser, Lord Lovat, to investigate lawless vandalism and the potential for trade in the Highlands. As they go they gradually probe the mystery of the death of Paul Macmaster, Aeneas's father, a Jacobite, who was alleged to have been killed at the Battle of Glenshiel in 1719. As the plot unravels, however, it turns out that he is not the casualty of a romantic cause but, in fact, the victim of a sordid murder by an unscrupulous and greedy "friend", Alexander Duncanson, who by guile and treachery has been able to acquire Paul's estate, Drimdorran. Suspense as to the whereabouts and method of the killing is maintained to the very last page when, after the sudden death of the murderer, Ninian, using his finely honed skills of deduction, discovers the evidence of Paul's burial and the dirk which was used to strike the fatal blow in the walled up fireplace of the doocot (dovecote) in Inveraray, the place where the mystery started.

The New Road, however, is not merely a thrilling 18th century detective story and murder mystery. It is much more than this. It builds on real historical characters such as General George Wade, Captain Edmund Burt, Col of Barisdale, Lord Lovat and Duncan Forbes of Culloden. It does not espouse the predictable sympathies of Jacobite romance but is told from the point of view of the pro-

The New Road

Hanoverian, anti-Jacobite House of Argyll, in this respect following Violet Jacob's novel *Flemington* (1911). As we accompany the inexperienced Aeneas on his journey north we are confronted with and helped to interpret some of the forces that shaped the history of modern Highland Scotland. Although there are regrets for the end of the old Highland way of life, the total thrust of the book shows a very positive direction for the future of Scotland, a Scotland in which the divide between Highland and Lowland can be healed.

2. HISTORICAL BACKGROUND

The Jacobites were so named for their allegiance to the Stuart King James VII of Scotland and II of England and his son James who was often known as the "Old Pretender". (Latin *Jacobus* means James.) They sought to restore the Stuarts to the throne after they had been removed in favour of William of Orange and his Hanoverian successors. They suffered a major setback in 1715 at the Battle of Sheriffmuir.

In 1719 a further attempt to restore the Stuarts was backed by Spain and a two-pronged attack was launched on England and Scotland. The England-bound fleet was scattered in a storm. The Scottish fleet with its Spanish soldiers reached Eilean Donan Castle at Lochalsh. Further support, however, was limited and, although the Jacobite forces held a superior position, they squandered their advantages and were defeated at Shiel Bridge by the Government forces under General Wightman. (In the story Paul Macmaster was supposed to have been one of the Jacobite troops and to have been drowned in Loch Duich after this battle.)

In order to prevent the recurrence of Jacobite risings north of the Border, General George Wade was appointed commander-in-chief of the British armed forces in Scotland. His job was to demilitarise the clans and to keep the peace. Part of his strategy for doing this was to provide a network of military roads connecting Inverness in the north with the Lowlands. The most obvious of these is the current A9 to Inverness which follows the line of Wade's road. Another peacekeeping device was the establishment of private militias or watches, but these, like Col of Barisdale's in the novel, quickly deteriorated into gangs of blackmailers and extortionists.

Simon Fraser, Lord Lovat, was the most powerful man in the Highlands. He had previously been an active Jacobite but in the 1715 Rising he had taken the government side and appeared to maintain this stance thereafter, although his position in the 1745 Rising was extremely dubious and led to his execution. He was more interested in maintaining his own power and hegemony in the north than allegiance to any other party. Neil Munro will have got much of the atmosphere of Lovat's Castle Dounie and its inhabitants from Burt's *Letters from the North of Scotland* (1754). The author of these, Captain Edmund Burt, is himself fictionalised in Chapter XVIII of *The New Road*.

Duncan Forbes of Culloden, the Lord Advocate, was the government's most powerful legal figure in Scotland. He was completely loyal to the government but was a Highlander himself and had the reputation of being extremely fair, even to Jacobites, and always stood up for Scottish interests in the British state. During the period of the novel, however, by far the most powerful political figure and supporter of the British government in Scotland was John, 2nd Duke of Argyll. He was made Duke of Greenwich and was also known as Red John of the Battles. He had led the government army at Sheriffmuir in 1715. Much of his time necessarily had to be spent in England and abroad. His Scottish and domestic affairs were handled by his brother Archibald, Earl of Islay. Although we never actually meet either of these two latter characters in the novel we are constantly kept aware of their power and influence.

3. STRUCTURE AND PLOT SUMMARY

The novel falls into five sections: the mysterious happenings at the doocot; the journey of Ninian and Aeneas to the north; events in Inverness and Castle Dounie and the involvement of Lord Lovat; the kidnapping of Aeneas aboard the *Wayward Lass*; the return of the main characters to Inveraray and resolution of the mystery of Paul's death. It opens and closes at the scene of the mystery – the doocot. Like *John Splendid* much of the story takes the form of the journey of the two main characters. They both set out on official business but inadvertently begin to probe the mystery of Paul Macmaster's death. Ironically, the further they go from home the more they penetrate the mystery of Paul's disappearance which was organised from and concluded in Inveraray.

Section I: Mystery at the Doocot (Chapters I–V)

Aeneas Macmaster is tutor to both Margaret, the daughter of Sandy Duncanson, the owner of the Drimdorran estate, and William, son of Lord Islay, the powerful brother of MacCailean Mòr, the Duke of Argyll. When he arrives at Drimdorran to give them their evening lesson they are absent. He is told by Duncanson's servant, the Muileach [a person from the island of Mull] that they have gone to the riverside. As he makes his way there he sees a light in the old doocot and assumes he will find them both in it. Margaret, however, is there on her own and she shows him a snuffbox on which there is a miniature portrait of a lady. Suddenly Aeneas hears someone outside. Eventually the person opens the door, sighs deeply and leaves without giving any clue of identity. Aeneas sets off for home but realises he still has the snuffbox. He returns with it and Margaret snatches it from him.

The narrator informs us of the political situation. Inveraray has become very much a Lowland town embracing the politics of the Duke of Argyll. He is one of the most powerful men in Scotland although he is not seen very frequently in his castle home at Inveraray. His brother Lord Islay manages most of the local affairs and in his absence Sandy Duncanson, who is the Duke's Baron-Bailie, takes charge. In many ways he has executive control of the Highlands. We are then introduced to Aeneas's Uncle Alan-Iain-Alain Og. He is a merchant who believes that the Jacobite Highland chiefs can be controlled and pacified by trade and the sale of luxury goods. Aeneas lives with Alan and his vivacious Lowland wife Annabel. Alan fears that Drimdorran is angry with Aeneas because he appears to be interested in his daughter Margaret. He clearly wants her to marry Will, Lord Islay's son.

Aeneas decides to visit Ninian Macgregor Campbell to see if he can shed light on the identity of the mysterious intruder at the doocot. Ninian is grandly called MacCailean Mòr's Messenger-at-Arms, although "government spy" might be a more accurate description of his occupation. He is a shrewd and fearless operator who knows the Highlands intimately. He is also superstitious. Ninian informs Aeneas that he is being sent on a mission to the north to investigate arms smuggling, blackmail and vandalism on the new road which is being built by General George Wade between Stirling and Inverness. The Duke of Argyll believes that the vandalism has been highly orchestrated and wants information. Ninian, however, suspects that Duncanson is jealous that he has been chosen for this work. He wants Aeneas to accompany him on his journey. He also tells Aeneas that Duncanson is very angry with him. The only reason that Aeneas can think of for this is that he was unable to teach his lesson earlier in the evening.

At 5am the Muileach summons Aeneas to Duncanson's presence. He passes him a note from Margaret saying that Aeneas is not to mention the doocot incident. Drimdorran accuses Aeneas of having William sent into town in order to have the opportunity of being alone with Margaret. He sacks him for being neglectful of his teaching duty but it is clear that he suspects Aeneas of stealing the keys for his desk and searching it. As he leaves, Margaret manages to tell him that she had organised Will's departure so that she could inspect the doocot. She promises to explain Aeneas's innocence in this matter to her father – but never does. (This is the last time that we meet this lively character.)

Aeneas's uncle Alan believes Drimdorran dismissed Aeneas because he suspects a liaison between Margaret and Aeneas. He then explains that the Drimdorran estate used to belong to his father Paul but that Duncanson eventually took possession of it as security for Paul's debts, accrued whilst he was away fighting for the Jacobite cause. Alan now wants to make Aeneas a merchant like himself. He sees trade as exciting and conveys this enthusiasm to his nephew. He encourages him to join Ninian on his expedition and warns him of the wickedness of Simon Fraser, Lord Lovat.

Ninian is keen to take Aeneas with him but is anxious to know why Drimdorran is angry with Aeneas, and ascertains that his friendship with Margaret seems to be the cause. He senses that Duncanson would use any excuse to stop his expedition, so they must be very careful. To prevent Drimdorran finding out that they are going together they agree to travel by different routes and to rendezvous at Bridge of Orchy. Janet, Ninian's daughter, for whom Aeneas obviously has feelings, is delighted that Aeneas will accompany her father.

The doocot is clearly of special significance in the story. We do not know the identity of the mysterious person who halts at its door while Margaret and Aeneas are inside, nor do we know the identity of the lady whose miniature portrait is on the snuffbox. Duncanson's anger seems disproportionate to Aeneas's apparent crime of failing to teach his evening lesson and we wonder if there is another, deeper, reason for his rage. We also see part of the Government/Campbell strategy for the pacification of the Highlands – the establishment of trade and commerce.

Section II: The Journey North (Chapters VI–XIII)

Aeneas proceeds north to Bridge of Orchy. At the inn there he meets Ninian who orders him into their room before he is recognised by the man who accompanied him to take his horse back to Inveraray. Ninian tells Aeneas that Duncanson wanted to know where Aeneas was going and has also accused him of stealing a snuffbox. Ninian wants to know all the details of the fateful evening and Aeneas provides these. Ninian now relates how he had been speaking to Drimdorran that evening. He got very angry when he saw that his desk had been searched and left

Ninian for about twenty minutes. Ninian noticed that there was a light in the doocot at this time, so there is no doubt that Drimdorran was the mysterious intruder on Margaret and Aeneas. Now Drimdorran can accuse Aeneas of a crime (stealing the snuffbox) without having to implicate his daughter and jeopardise her marriage prospects with Will Campbell. It is, therefore, all the more important that Ninian's man does not know that Aeneas is at Bridge of Orchy. However, the man has already recognised Aeneas's horse, so Aeneas's whereabouts will soon be known to Duncanson.

They set off on the rest of their journey on foot. While fishing in the river Orchy they are passed by a galloping horseman who completely ignores their greeting. They proceed on their journey but are unable to summon the ferry across Loch Tulla, only to find out later that the ferryman has had instructions not to pick them up. After a bizarre encounter with a Macintyre on the track to Loch Etive they reach the inn at Buachaille Etive (Kingshouse) in Glencoe. The daughter of the innkeeper warns Ninian that Niall of Succoth and others are pursuing him. A company of men approach. Ninian identifies their leader as the notorious and superficially educated Col of Barisdale. He is captain of a Watch who makes his money through extortion. Aeneas and Ninian don Highland dress to conceal their identities. Aeneas tells Barisdale that they are Macmasters of Drimdorran. Barisdale informs Aeneas that many years before he had a fencing bout with his father Paul at Castle Dounie and that Aeneas is his double. Later Ninian says they will have to leave soon because Aeneas may have given the game away by admitting that they come from Drimdorran – a place too near Inveraray. Ninian is afraid that Barisdale wants to tail him and render his expedition useless.

A *creach* or herd of stolen cattle is brought in led by a man purporting to be a Macgregor but who is in fact a lieutenant of Col. He tells Ninian that "some Big One" has put the country against him and advises him to leave east by Ben Alder at 5am next morning.

Realising this is a trap they leave even earlier, heading

west and over the Devil's Staircase and north to the river Spean and the pass of Corryarrick. Ninian wants to know whom Col is working for.

At midnight they seek hospitality in the village of Druimbeg on Loch Laggan which is populated only by women and children. In one house a woman gives them food because Ninian tells her he is a Macgregor but refuses them a place to sleep. She advises them to leave before the men return. All the doors in the village are barred against them. They eventually find shelter in a large building in which they find scores of broken Dutch muskets. Ninian is disturbed by voices and looks out to see men in fighting gear carrying a chest. Later he is wakened by the tolling of a bell. They are in a Catholic chapel and Aeneas has unwittingly pulled the bell rope! They make a run for it to the shore of Loch Laggan to avoid capture. They are pursued by four men, two of whom Ninian deals with and a third is shot and killed (or so he thinks) by Aeneas. They cross the loch in leaky boat. Ninian honours Aeneas for having achieved his first killing by placing the tip of his sword on his head but Aeneas is disgusted by the barbarity of this custom. Ninian is in no doubt that the Loch Laggan incident will come to the ears of Duncanson and that he will now know for certain that Aeneas is with him.

The travellers now proceed to the Pass of Corryarrick where Captain Leggatt and his soldiers are engineering a section of new road. Work has been held up because the soldiers' wages have been stolen. Leggatt believes that Simon Fraser, Lord Lovat, is responsible for the theft and the vandalism of the road and seeks Ninian's help. Ninian tells Leggatt of the chest (the soldiers' wages) in Druimbeg. He sets off at once to retrieve it. Ninian is certain that their names will no longer be connected with this incident because Leggatt will want the credit for himself.

Ninian writes to Lord Islay telling him that a Jacobite rising in the north is unlikely. The weapons discovered are useless but are advantageous to the local people because they can hand them in to the government and receive payment for them. What is important is to find out who is financing this scam. He also says that someone set

Barisdale after him. He wonders whether to include mention of Aeneas in the letter. Aeneas had assured him that he did not have the snuffbox and Ninian feels that something more than a liaison between his daughter Margaret and Aeneas is upsetting Duncanson. Leggatt comes back from Druimbeg with the news that no one had been killed in the skirmish – to Aeneas's delight! Leggatt has the wages chest and the muskets and takes the credit for the wounding of the man Aeneas shot.

The mention by Barisdale of a previous fencing bout between himself and Paul Macmaster increases the mystery surrounding Paul's disappearance. The encounter with the bully Barisdale and his extortion racket in Glencoe begins the process of Aeneas's disillusionment with the glamour of the Highlands and the Jacobite chiefs. This is intensified by his disgust at Ninian's celebration of his "blooding" at Loch Laggan. We start to wonder at the purpose of the consignment of broken muskets. Although Ninian and Aeneas are now a considerable distance from Inveraray the reader begins to suspect the hand of Duncanson may be influencing their affairs.

Section III: Inverness and Lord Lovat (Chapters XIV–XVIII)

They reach Inverness. Ninian tells Aeneas to put the money given him by his uncle for trade into the hands of his agent Saul Mackay. Ninian visits Duncan Forbes, the Lord Advocate, in his house at Culloden. He tells him about the Dutch muskets retrieved at Druimbeg. For Forbes the big question is: who is financing the importing of these obsolete weapons? Forbes then turns the conversation to the presence of Aeneas with Ninian which gives Ninian the opportunity to discuss his real reason for coming to see him – the death of Paul Macmaster. Ninian tells Forbes that Barisdale claimed to have had a fencing bout with Paul at Castle Dounie, Lord Lovat's stronghold. This was after the Battle of Glenshiel and so Paul had not been drowned in Loch Duich after the battle, which is what everybody had been led to believe. Barisdale had also told Ninian that

The New Road

Paul had died abroad. Forbes advises Ninian to concentrate on his official business for the Duke of Argyll and not to stir up the past.

Ninian goes to Castle Dounie to see Lord Lovat on the pretext of delivering a letter from his daughter Janet to Lovat's wife Primrose Campbell, the Duke of Argyll's niece. She is very unhappy and obviously ill-treated. Lovat asks why Ninian has come north. He explains it is to investigate vandalism of the new road and trafficking in arms. Lovat, although once a Jacobite, protests his loyalty to the British Government. Ninian explains that his progress north had been impeded by Barisdale. Lovat curses Barisdale. He is clearly not his friend. He also confirms the duel between Paul Macmaster and Barisdale.

Aeneas is excited by the prospect of commerce. His uncle's agent Mackay, however, would not look after his money for him because there was too much! Ninian confesses that he had been sure that Lovat was the "Big One" behind all the vandalism on the road and their own misfortunes. Now he knows he is not. He clearly did not put Barisdale up to any of this. He tells Aeneas that his father was not drowned or killed at the Battle of Glenshiel and they would return to Lovat to ask him more about the fencing bout. He feels that something more mysterious than drowning befell Paul Macmaster.

Aeneas attracts a great deal of attention in Inverness because of the amount of money he has with him. In the inn where they are staying Ninian produces two hanks of string. One of these is a mass of tangle: this represents his confusion surrounding Paul Macmaster's death. The other hank is a neatly rolled stick of twine: this represents Ninian's almost completed official business. They go back to Castle Dounie and ask Lovat for more information about Paul Macmaster. At a drinking party he explains that he had given sanctuary to Paul for a month after the Battle of Glenshiel, even although he himself was on the side of the British Government. He tells Aeneas that he looks like his mother because Paul had shown him a portrait of her. Paul did not leave Castle Dounie for Inveraray; Duncanson had sent him money to go abroad! He left on one of Lovat's horses with a silver mounted saddle, heading for Perth or Stirling. The horse and its trappings were not returned to Lovat but Duncanson paid him their value. Duncanson told Lovat that Paul had died in France a year later. Lovat is surprised that Aeneas and his uncle Alan did not know this. During this discussion we learn that Lovat does not wish the lot of his people improved in any way. This ensures that he maintains his autocratic authority over them. At this point the post arrives although we do not learn the contents of Lovat's mail. Lovat asks for Ninian and Aeneas's address in Inverness.

It is now clear that Paul was not killed at Glenshiel. The mystery surrounding his death deepens. It is also clear that Lovat is no friend of Barisdale and it was clearly not Lovat who used Barisdale to impede the progress of Ninian and Aeneas. Although on the Government side, Lovat had sheltered Paul and genuinely believed that he had gone to France and died there a year later – but he had got this information from none other than Duncanson.

Aeneas's disillusion with the romance of the Highlands is completed when he samples the licentious and riotous behaviour of Lovat and his friends in Castle Dounie and realises that the powerful chief has no desire to improve the lot of his people but wishes to keep them in subservience and dependency so that they have no choice but to support his power-base in the north.

The letter which arrives in Chapter XVIII (pp185–6) is of great importance, although its contents are not yet revealed to us.

Section IV: Kidnapped (Chapters XIX–XXVII)

Ninian and Aeneas return to their inn in Inverness. There they are attacked by four men. Aeneas is kidnapped and Ninian is captured in a trammel net and is knocked senseless. When Ninian comes to he cuts himself out and makes his way to a hiding place beside the Bunchrew Burn, and then visits Duncan Forbes at Culloden. They deduce that the attack was masterminded by Lovat because Ninian knows that he is responsible for the Dutch muskets and will

The New Road

report this to Islay. Ninian then meets his daughter Janet who has come north in search of him. Margaret Duncanson had told her that he had been drowned in Loch Laggan and her father had got this information from one of Barisdale's men. Now Ninian knows for sure that Lovat is not the "Big One" who has been tracking and obstructing them: it is Duncanson. Duncanson also knows all Lovat's doings because all Lovat's correspondence to Islay goes through his hands. Clearly Duncanson is playing a double game.

Janet is furious that Ninian has lost Aeneas. Ninian also clearly realises that Duncanson is not just concerned about Ninian going north; he is also afraid that Aeneas will find some information about his father's death when he is in the Inverness area.

Janet decides to go and see Primrose Campbell. When she returns she tells Forbes that Lovat treats Primrose very badly. She also says that Ninian and Aeneas were no problem to Lovat until a letter arrived at Castle Dounie. Something in that letter made it necessary for Lovat to try to capture them. Forbes wants to know the contents of that letter. (pp227–8)

Ninian catches sight of three sailors who have been trailing him. He now realises that throughout their journey north it is Aeneas who has been pursued, not himself. He thinks that Duncanson and Lovat believe Aeneas saw something in Duncansons's desk which incriminates them – although Aeneas was quite unaware of this! Ninian deduces that Aeneas has been captured by sailors and that he is probably on board the *Wayward Lass* which is moored offshore in the Beauly Firth. Forbes has the boat searched twice but the searchers fail to find him. Janet says that she has always suspected Duncanson and felt he wanted Aeneas's destruction. Forbes also points out to Ninian that Janet is clearly in love with Aeneas.

In order to locate Aeneas, Ninian lets himself be captured by the men who are trailing him. They take him aboard the *Wayward Lass* where he meets Aeneas. Ninian gets one of the sailors to admit that this kidnapping is all Lovat's doing. In order to enable them to escape he manages to sever all but the last strand of the anchor cable. It eventually snaps and in the chaos and fighting which follows they commandeer a boat and, with another prisoner, a Fraser, they escape.

When they reach shore Fraser runs off as soon as possible. He had had no idea why he had been captured but 12 years before he had been in Lovat's service and was among the Frasers fighting at Glenshiel. Forbes commands Ninian and Aeneas to leave at once. Ninian's official business has been completed and his presence in the north is only stirring up trouble, more so now that he has scuttled the ship. Forbes wants them to go by coach down the New Road next evening. Ninian, however, insists on going to visit Fraser in his home at Muir of Ord before he leaves.

Ironically it is at the furthest point of their journey north that Ninian realises that the cause of their harassment is lurking at home in Inveraray – Duncanson! It is also clear that it is only when a letter arrives from Duncanson that Lovat turns nasty on them and organises their kidnapping. Fraser will provide the final link between the death of Paul and Duncanson.

Section V: Return to Inveraray and Resolution (Chapters XXVIII–XXXVII)

Although Ninian does not track down Fraser himself he appears to have found out something useful from his wife. Ninian, Aeneas and Janet journey south down the New Road by coach from Daviot (near Inverness). Janet tells Aeneas that Duncanson became very frightened when he learned that Aeneas had gone to Inverness. Aeneas now thinks that whatever Duncanson believes he saw in the doocot has been the root of all their trouble. They return to Inveraray.

Duncanson seems to become crazed at night-time and has his entire house lit with candles. He appears to have had a stroke. He is startled when Ninian enters as he believes him to have drowned in Loch Laggan but is relieved when Ninian tells him that Aeneas had been kidnapped. Ninian tells him Aeneas had never looked in his desk and did not steal the snuffbox, but that his daughter Margaret had indeed taken the keys for the doocot from it. Duncanson clearly realises that he has jumped to the wrong conclusion and that Margaret has ruined things for him. Ninian is surprised that there is a tartan screen across the window overlooking the doocot.

Ninian meets Alan who has been to Laggan in search of them. He explains to him that Duncanson is a double agent and would now fall foul of MacCailean and Islay. Lovat and Duncanson were both involved in the importation of the Dutch muskets, Lovat in order to maintain his power and Duncanson for the money. He also tells him that the letter which Duncanson wrote to Lovat was the reason for the kidnapping. In it he told Lovat that the travellers were getting too close to unravelling the mystery of Paul's death. (p304)

Ninian and Alan join the others at Alan's house. Aeneas wants to hear his father's story from the beginning. Alan tells him that Duncanson came to Inveraray and took over his employer's law firm. He courted the woman who was to become Paul's wife and Aeneas's mother. He appeared to be a good friend of Paul Macmaster. Paul's wife died a year after their marriage. Paul then went to fight for the Jacobite cause and Duncanson succeeded in acquiring Drimdorran.

Annabel wonders if Paul is still alive but Janet and Ninian are sure he is dead – although there is as yet no proof. Then a message comes from Duncanson asking to see Aeneas.

Aeneas meets Ninian at the doocot and reports his conversation with Duncanson. He said that Duncanson claimed to have persuaded Paul to leave for France and sent letters to him there. He claimed Paul died a double agent, having given away Jacobite secrets. Ninian does not believe this at all and is sure that the answer lies in the doocot. He is sure that it was Aeneas's presence in the doocot on the evening of the missed lesson that gave him his stroke. Duncanson had had the doocot boarded up to keep out the pigeons and, therefore, to stop people coming there. He asks Aeneas if he can smell soot.

Later that evening Ninian sees Duncanson trying to get into his old home in the town. He is obviously deranged. Before going home he visits the doocot. Ninian follows him but is too late to find out what he is looking for. Next morning he concludes his official mission by writing his report for the Duke.

Aeneas examines a barrel of papers belonging to his father and finds an accounts ledger which has clearly been falsified in Duncanson's favour. It also appears that Duncanson has no title deed giving him the right to Drimdorran – only a scrap of paper signed by Paul pledging the estate to Duncanson for security. And this too may have been forged by Duncanson! Ninian goes to the doocot to watch Duncanson's next move but he never comes. He dies. Ninian returns to Drimdorran and discovers Duncanson had received a letter from Lovat saying that Aeneas and Ninian had left the north and that they had discussed the matter of Paul's death with Fraser who had been kidnapped with them. The shock of this reference to Fraser kills him. Ninian then discovers the snuffbox. The portrait on it is, of course, of Paul's wife. How did Duncanson get it? Paul would never have parted with it.

Ninian is convinced that Paul had been killed in the parish of Inveraray. He had discovered from Fraser's wife that Paul had used him as a messenger to take a letter to Duncanson telling him of his intended visit to collect money and see his son before going to France. He also took Duncanson's reply back to Paul arranging to meet him alone in Glen Aray. Ninian concludes that Duncanson killed Paul to make sure that he would retain Drimdorran and avoid being accused of other crimes. He must have taken the snuffbox from his corpse. Paul rode down from Inverness on Lovat's horse with the silver-mounted saddle.

Ninian goes to the doocot once more to complete his investigations. It seems that there was once a fireplace in the doocot. This is the clue Ninian has been looking for. Meantime Janet and Aeneas confirm their love for one another. Janet's intuition tells her that Duncanson met Paul and murdered him in the doocot. She is right – Ninian returns and addresses Aeneas as Drimdorran, his righful title. He has come into his inheritance. Duncanson had bricked up the fireplace leaving in it Paul's body, the silver-mounted saddle and the dirk with which he had killed him. The doocot is a tomb and the curtain on Duncanson's window prevented him having to look on the site of Paul's murder.

The disintegration of Duncanson is graphically described as guilt and helplessness engulf him. The knowledge that Ninian is on the point of exposing him as a political double-dealer and the murderer of Paul is too much for him to endure and he collapses and dies. Aeneas receives his rightful inheritance – he is now Drimdorran – and he and Janet confirm their mutual love. The certain proof of Paul's murder is provided dramatically by Ninian on the last page of the novel.

4. THEMES AND CHARACTERS

On a first reading *The New Road* is above all a historical murder mystery. Closer inspection, however, reveals that it encompasses important themes which examine some of the forces which shape modern Scotland and, more particularly, the Scottish Highlands.

(1) Theme of murder mystery: what happened to Paul Macmaster?

The surface theme is Aeneas's search for his Jacobite father. The novel is 18th century crime fiction and Ninian Macgregor Campbell is a perceptive detective. The fact that Ninian is a Macgregor by birth (he had adopted Campbell as a surname for reasons of political expediency) is relevant here. The Macgregors were an outlawed and persecuted clan who had to struggle to survive. Ninian's Macgregor ancestry has sharpened his wits and resourcefulness and equipped him for the job of Messenger-at-Arms – which is, in effect, that of a government spy.

The story opens at the mysterious doocot. Duncanson's rage at Aeneas for failing to conduct a lesson for his daughter that evening and for being in the doocot with her is wildly disproportionate to any misdemeanour he may be thought guilty of. As Aeneas and Ninian go north on their respective missions they keep meeting obstacles and obstructions. Ninian assumes that they are suffering this harassment because of his position as Messenger-at-Arms to MacCailean Mòr, the Duke of Argyll. In fact the target of this persecution is Aeneas. Paradoxically, the further he goes north the closer he is to finding out the truth about his father's disappearance. At the furthest point from home, Castle Dounie, they learn from Lovat that Paul was not drowned at the Battle of Glenshiel. He is supposed to have gone to France. He never got there. The mystery is solved only when they return to the doocot. Suspense is maintained to the very last page when Ninian reveals that Duncanson murdered Paul in the doocot and buried him in the bricked up fireplace along with the dirk he had used to kill him. The doocot is a tomb. Ninian's skill as a detective is symbolised by the use of the two hanks of twine which he unravels as he solves the clues to the crimes in the story.

(2) Theme of Disillusionment

Like Scott's great novels *Waverley* and *Rob Roy*, *The New Road* is set at a time of major change – the period after the Battles of Sheriffmuir and Glenshiel and the construction of Wade's famous roads which were built in response to these with the intention of subjugating the Highlands. Into this situation is thrust **Aeneas Macmaster**, a young man of twenty-two who, like Edward Waverley in Scott's novel, is hypersensitive and sentimental:

> his heart was all in pictures and in poetry –
> very pretty things no doubt, but scarcely with
> a living in them. (p47)

Like Waverley, he too is in love with his own distorted romantic view of the Highlands. He is sacked by Duncanson, ostensibly for neglecting his duties as tutor to Duncanson's daughter and ward, but in reality because he was coming dangerously close to stumbling on the circumstances of his father's murder. His uncle, Alan-Iain-

The New Road

Alain Og, suggests that he accompany Ninian Campbell who, as Messenger-at-Arms to the Duke of Argyll, was about to make a journey to Inverness to investigate reports of gun running, cattle thieving and vandalism of the New Road. Alan suggests that Aeneas take this opportunity to assess the business potential of the North now that the New Road is nearing completion. At first the prospect of a commercial expedition seems dull and boring but when his uncle describes it as "Adventure" (p51) his whole attitude changes:

> Now to his uncle's great astonishment, he leapt on Blaeu [an atlas], and with his chest upon the parts he knew, he peered, transported, on that legendary region of the boisterous clans, still in the state of ancient Gaul, and with Gaul's customs. The very names of castles, passes, straths, misspelled, entranced him; everything was strange and beckoning. Moreover, it had been the country of his father's wanderings, somewhere there his father had been slain, somewhere there was buried. (p51)

They set off on what for Aeneas, like Waverley, will be a journey of disillusionment and education. First, they meet the petty chieftain and Master of a Watch, **Col of Barisdale**, who clearly intends mischief against them. He is a bombastic bully with laughable pretensions to urbane culture and scholarship. For Aeneas he is the first indication that his romantic notion of the Highlands might be false:

> All at once it came upon him that his glamoured notion of the North was just a kind of poetry in himself; it vexed him to reflect that, after all, the heroes of the *ceilidh* tales – the chiefs and caterans – were, like enough, but men of wind as this one seemed. (p85)

Furthermore, once Aeneas has seen the unscrupulous way Col, who is supposed as Captain of a Watch to protect farmers against cattle reiving or the *creach*, takes a herd of

Glen Lyon cattle for himself, he is further disappointed because another romantic notion has been destroyed:

> Till now, the customs of the North, as he had heard of them, high-coloured with imagination, had appeared to have a kind of gallantry, and now the foray – most inspiring of them all, as having in it something of adventure and the risk of war – was shown as commonplace and mean. (p97)

Aeneas's disgust increases when Ninian honours him by laying the tip of his sword blade on his head in accordance with Highland custom after he has been "blooded" by shooting dead (as he believes) a Macdonald at Druimbeg. At this he is physically sick and exclaims:

> "Everything's destroyed for me! ... The stories have been lies, and we have aye been beasts, and cloak it up in poetry." (p115)

When he reaches Inverness, acting as his uncle's agent he meets a number of petty chiefs and is utterly disillusioned by them, seeing them to be more grasping and acquisitive than the meanest merchant:

> From these proud petty chiefs he got his last illumination of the North as glamoured mainly to the eye of fancy, and a gleam went off the hills for him as slips the sunset off the heather ... he found that just as Barisdale below his leather coat was but a bellows, so these men of family, for all their show of native ancient pomp and ritual, were more the merchantmen than Alan-Iain-Alain Og. They haggled like to fishwives on the price of salt and salmon crops, and pickled beef, and timber. (p171)

His greatest and most powerful disillusion comes, however, in his meeting with the most powerful chieftain in the North – **MacShimi, Simon Fraser, Lord Lovat**. In Castle Dounie he hears this chieftain, in his specious paternalism to his people, treat them with utter contempt with these words:

> "Here is a healthy and contented people bruicking and enjoying every comfort fitted to their state, secure of the invasion of those desperate and levelling ideas that in other places have played havoc with the loyalty of commons and reduced authority of chiefs."
> (p184)

He even refuses them schools. As long as the Highland aristocracy's children are educated according to their needs he sees no need to educate the common people:

> "My people always have what fits them best in their condition – schooling of the winter and the blast, rough fare, the hills to strive wi', and the soil to break. They need no more, except their swords and skill to use them."
> (p184)

Not surprisingly Aeneas is outraged at the sheer barbarism of this and describes it as "blasphemy". And, as if this were not enough, he also learns that Lovat keeps his sad and dispirited wife **Primrose Campbell** a virtual prisoner in Castle Dounie.

Like Waverley, he has had the veil lifted from his eyes and he now sees the Jacobite Highlands for what they really are. The only aspect of them which has remained true to his earlier notion of them is the image of his father. **Paul Macmaster** was not the corrupt double agent Duncanson made him out to be. The Duke of Argyll himself, although Paul's political enemy, tells Ninian that Paul would never have betrayed his friends.

Over and above Aeneas's personal disillusionment the overwhelming impression is given of corruption and barbarity among the rulers of Highland society. By any objective standard Barisdale is a thug. Ninian uncovers Lovat's cunning ploy of importing obsolete guns from Holland so that the clansmen can sell them to the Government under the Disarming Act while the good weapons are kept in the thatch of the houses, thus enabling him to remain the most powerful man in the Highlands and, if need be, ready to take part in another rising. As Ninian says,

> "He wants to keep the real stuff in the thatch; he doesna want the North disarmed no more than he wants roads and schools. So long's the North has gun and claymore ready, Simon is king beyond the Spey." (p303)

Sandy Duncanson is a nefarious double dealer, outwardly professing allegiance to Argyll, while, mainly for money, clandestinely in league with Lovat. His family is from Gunna, a small, barren and rocky islet between Col and Tiree. Col was a rebellious place whilst Tiree belonged to civilised Argyll. Duncanson, or Maclean as he was then known, chose to live in whichever of those places suited his needs. The meanness of Gunna symbolises Duncanson's own character whilst his lack of loyalty to either Col or Tiree is symptomatic of the greed which was to characterise his whole life. Significantly both Lovat and Duncanson are described as spiders in a web who cunningly control the dark deeds of the Highlands. Paul Macmaster, on the other hand, is an honourable Jacobite but we are given the impression that he was rather feckless and seduced by a romantic dream rather than a realistic conviction.

The arbitrary power of the chiefs is again endorsed in their ability to dictate their clansmen's religion as Ninian tells Aeneas when they are in Druimbeg:

> "Ye'll mind we're in among a lot of heathens, no' right sure yet whether they are Protestant or Papist till the chief of them comes round to tell them wi' a yellow stick." (p111)

Meanwhile Alan-Iain-Alain Og suggests that it is the chieftain class who are the cause of the troubles in the Highlands:

> "It's no the common people, mind! – the poor and faithful clansmen – but their lairds and chiefs I'm after, them your father marched wi'

The New Road

in his folly, blind to their self-interest, thinking they were only out for James." (p52)

This insight into the behaviour of the chiefs anticipates the later Scottish novelist Neil Gunn's similar identification of them as the major weakness in the 18th century Highland society. He targets their changed relationship with their people (albeit after the battle of Culloden in 1746) as a primary cause of the Highland Clearances in *Butcher's Broom*,[2] whilst the sympathy for the common people, although only just touched on in Munro, anticipates the more extensive treatment of this theme in Neil Gunn's *Butcher's Broom* (1934), Fionn MacColla's *And the Cock Crew* (1945) and Iain Crichton Smith's *Consider the Lilies* (1968).

(3) Theme of Regeneration

Against the disillusionment of the sensitive young hero figure and the more generalised criticism of Highland society must be set the regenerative aspects of the novel. As mentioned before, *The New Road* flouts the usual convention in novels dealing with the Jacobite period by presenting the case, not from the Stuart side, but from the Hanoverian perspective through **MacCailein Mòr, the Duke of Argyll**,[3] and his brother **Islay**. These two figures are never actually encountered in the novel although we are constantly conscious of their influential presence in the background as men who are Enlightenment "improvers", men who are carrying on the tradition of peaceful commerce in Argyll introduced by Gillesbeg Gruamach in *John Splendid*. They stand for civilised values and are presented as acting in Scotland's best interests. Likewise the Lord Advocate, **Duncan Forbes of Culloden**, is presented as a reasonable person torn between his instinctive loyalties to the past and the need for civilisation in the modern world. Most interesting of all, however, in this regard is the highly charismatic and stable character of **Ninian Macgregor Campbell**, *beachdair* (scout) and Messenger-at-Arms to MacCailein Mòr. It has frequently been remarked that *The New Road* resembles Stevenson's

Kidnapped in that Ninian and Aeneas are counterparts to Alan Breck and David Balfour. At a superficial level this is true. But where Munro rings a skilful change is in placing his highly attractive, charismatic, perceptive and competent Alan Breck character, not on the side of the Stuarts, but on the side of Argyll. The mere act of doing this transforms the credibility and attractiveness of the Hanoverian side in the reader's eyes. Like Forbes, Ninian has great sympathy with the plight of the suffering Highlander because of his own persecuted Macgregor lineage but, nonetheless, his loyalty to MacCailein and his civilising values are beyond all question and in this he takes the reader with him.

Ninian's decency and warm personality are reinforced by his loyal and courageous daughter **Janet**. She makes the dangerous journey to Inverness alone to seek her father and Aeneas when she learns that they are in trouble. When there she also undertakes a hazardous visit to comfort her friend **Primrose Campbell**, the maltreated wife of Lord Lovat.

The regenerative impulse is intensified in the character of **Alan-Iain-Alain Og**. With his good-humoured, shrewd and "managing" Lowland wife **Annabel** he has provided a home for Aeneas since his father disappeared. He is a successful merchant who can now control his business throughout the country without leaving Inveraray. He is a Bailie and has gradually adopted all the external hallmarks of a Lowland burgess. Indeed, he has grown quite stout:

> Mercantile prosperity would seem to have an ill effect upon the trunk, in which the energy and elegance of men and women mainly centre, as they say, and he was grown a little heavy and deliberate in his movements. (p17)

He sees the North as an opportunity for trade and commerce and the New Road as the ideal means of accessing these new markets. Indeed, he has given Aeneas special instructions to evaluate its usefulness for his enterprise (p50). Like that other famous Bailie, Nicol Jarvie in Sir Walter Scott's *Rob Roy*, he sees trade as the logical and sensible way forward for a modern nation rather than

The New Road

an obsession with a romantic affection for the feuding of the past. He sees the operation of the modern man of business as an adventure just as the clan wars were adventures in the past:

> "It's just a bit of an adventure," said the Bailie. "That's the thing wi' me in business, otherwise it wasna worth a docken leaf!" (p51)

He believes with MacCailein, furthermore, that trade is the way to pacify and civilise the North:

> "That's right!" the Duke would say to him, with a jaunty step into the store among the coopers packing powdered sugar, tea and hops, silk cloths, tobacco-rolls and looking glasses, – "that's right, Bailie! keep tickling them with luxuries, and I'll guarantee you'll help to subjugate my savage Hielandmen far quicker than we'll do it with their Watches and dragoons." (p16)

But it is here he goes further than Nicol Jarvie, and the old unregenerate Highland temperament also shows itself. In addition to making money, trade with the Highland chiefs is his way of seeking vengeance for his brother Paul whom he considers they seduced into the Jacobite cause. By civilising them through trade and commerce he says,

> "... *I'm smashing them*, the very men that led my brother Paul astray. MacCailein and me! MacCailein and me! And now there's Marshal Wade and his bonny Road that's going to make the North a land for decent folk to live in! ... Once the New Road is finished, and the troopers and the guns and my carts on it, it's an end to the dominion o' the chiefs." (p52)

(4) Theme of The New Road

And this brings us to the New Road itself. It will penetrate a land previously impenetrable to all but the brave or foolhardy:

> Since roads had been in Scotland they had reached to Stirling, but at Stirling they had stopped, and on the castle rock the sentinel at nightfall saw the mists go down upon a distant land of bens and glens on which a cannon or a carriage wheel had never yet intruded. Only the bridle-paths to kirk and market, the drove-track on the shoulders of the hills! (p48)

Now all this is about to change. Wade's road, a considerable feat of engineering, will open up the country from Stirling to the Moray Firth and this will radically improve trade and transport and bring prosperity. But it is not just trade and transport that will change; it is a whole way of life that will alter, and this, for any native Gael, will be a matter for regret. As Ninian says the whole Gaelic way of life will change irretrievably:

> "I'm tellin' you that Road is goin' to be a rut that, once it's hammered deep enough, will be the poor Gael's grave!" (pp34–5)

and, of course, as **Duncan Forbes** inadvertently prophesies, it will transport the cannons that will suppress the Rising of '45 (pp278–9). Indeed, the process of change initiated by Wade's road goes on today as the North is relentlessly stripped of its Gaelic character.

The road then becomes a symbol of the union of Highlands and Lowlands, a symbol of prosperity, and a symbol of the new civilised values which MacCailein and Forbes are trying to introduce against the barbarity of Lovat and his supporters who have steadfastly organised the vandalism of the road to ensure their primitive hegemony. But even the humane Forbes, a Highlander himself with all the *dualchas* (heritage) of the true Gael, cannot see this change implemented without regret. His statement to Ninian sums up the situation:

> "The hearts of all of us are sometimes in the wilds. It's not so very long since we left them. But the end of all that sort of thing's at hand. The man who's going to put an end to it – to

The New Road 57

> you and Lovat and to me – yes, yes, to me! or the like of me, half fond of plot and strife and savagery, is Wade ... Ye saw the Road? That Road's the end of us! The Romans didna manage it; Edward didna manage it; but there it is at last, through to our vitals, and it's up wi' the ell-wand, down the sword! It may seem a queer thing for a law officer of the Crown to say, Mr Campbell, but I never was greatly taken wi' the ell-wand, and man, I liked the sword! At least it had some glitter." (p208)

(An ell-wand is a yardstick used by tailors and, therefore, a symbol of trade and commerce.)

The New Road, then, affirms a myth of regeneration. In Scott's *Waverley* Edward Waverley becomes charmed by the romantic but false glamour of the Highlands but in the end good sense prevails and he opts to return to the Hanoverian fold; likewise Aeneas has his eyes opened to the falseness of Highland chieftains and their superficial glamour. In Scott's *Rob Roy* the Jacobite cause is a romantic dream, but the true way forward in the modern world is through the sensible trade and commerce of Bailie Nicol Jarvie; likewise Alan-Iain-Alain Og and his nephew Aeneas Macmaster choose to pursue this route vigorously. And the key to this civilised prosperity is the New Road. Costs will have to be paid and there will be regrets, as Aeneas himself acknowledges (pp280–1), but the ell-wand is preferable to the sword for all its glitter; and the head, not the heart, determines that the New Road is the route to take despite the attractions of romance or nostalgia.

5. SETTING

The New Road opens and finishes at the doocot near Inveraray, the heart of the mystery of the story. As in *John Splendid*, Munro describes the new town built in the later eighteenth century which exists today rather than the older village to which the events of the story historically belong. Aeneas and Ninian travel north via Bridge of Orchy and

Glencoe. (The inn at Buachaille Etive is the site of the modern Kingshouse Hotel). Then they go through Glen Nevis (near Fort William) to Loch Laggan. After this they proceed north across the Corryarrick Pass where a new military road is being built and on to Inverness. They then proceed to Castle Dounie on the Beauly Firth where the riotous atmosphere mirrors the character of its owner, Simon Fraser, Lord Lovat. They return by coach on a completed section of military road from Daviot (near Inverness) to the south, the line of the current A9. Finally they reach Inveraray – and the doocot – where the mystery of Paul Macmaster's death is solved. (See map at the beginning of the novel.)

The landscape through which Aeneas and Ninian travel is rough and the going is slow. The times are troubled and fraught with danger as the encounters with Col of Barisdale and the kidnapping in Inverness illustrate. But the journey is more than a physically testing experience: it is also a learning experience. As he progresses on his way, Aeneas is disabused of his romantic notions of the Highlands and Highland chieftains. He begins to appreciate the civilisation, peace and prosperity which the New Road will bring. At a metaphorical level his own life has begun to take a more mature and practical New Road.

6. LANGUAGE AND STYLE

As in Munro's other Highland stories, in *The New Road* he maintains a style of language which creates the illusion for the reader that the main language of the novel is Gaelic. He achieves this by the frequent use of Gaelic idiom and syntax in his English and by the occasional inclusion of suitable Gaelic words. Again, too, he puts a fair number of Scots words into the mouths of his characters – appropriately, for this, rather than Standard English, would have been the language of their Lowland neighbours which Gaels would have heard and quickly learned.

The Gaelic atmosphere of this novel is also enriched by the inclusion of Highland superstition. Even the tough and experienced Ninian insists on carrying a Virgin Nut with

The New Road

him for good luck wherever he goes (although ironically he discovers he did not have it when he needed it most). This was a molucca bean, known in Uist and Barra as *Airne Mhoire*, "the kidney of Mary". The mark of a cross is faintly discernible on it and it was used as a charm against evil in the Highlands and Islands.

A further example of this type of superstitious behaviour occurs when Ninian is desperately searching for the kidnapped Aeneas. At Bunchrew Burn he stretches his hands to the east, then washes his face and declaims an *Ora Ceartais* (Invocation for Justice):

> Black is yon town yonder
> Black the folk therein
> I am the white swan,
> King above them.
>
> In the name of God I'll go,
> In the shape of deer or horse,
> Like the serpent and the sword,
> I'll sting them! (p205).

This cleansing ritual and the invocation declaimed (slightly adapted) are taken from Alexander Carmichael's *Carmina Gadelica*, a famous collection of Gaelic hymns and incantations which Munro clearly admired and which is one of the most important Gaelic texts of the early twentieth century.[4]

Finally, as in *John Splendid*, the language of *The New Road* is often very highly charged and emotive. A fine example of this occurs when the travellers are on their journey home. They sit down for a rest and from their vantage point see before them the Old Road and the New Road running side by side down the valley into Badenoch. Aeneas describes the scene before him in the following moving and elegiac words:

> "I could weep myself to think our past is there. Where men have walked are always left the shades of them – their spirits lingering. To your eyes and to mine is nothing on the old drove-road but grass and boulder, but if

> there's aught of the immortal in men's souls, there's the immortal likewise in their earthly acts. Our folk are on the old-drove road – the ghosts of them, the hunters and the tribes long-perished to the eye, *daoin'-uasail* and broken men. It's history! It means the end of many things, I doubt, not all to be despised, – the last stand of Scotland, and she destroyed. And yet – and yet, this New Road will some day be the Old Road, too, with ghosts on it and memories ..." (pp280–1)

Here the contrast between the ordinary and the immortal, the listing of local inhabitants from earliest times and the contrast between old and new, produce an elegiac tone which emphasises the price that Scotland, and the Highlands in particular, will have to pay for progress. The repetition of the phrase "and yet", however, underlines the irony that this progress – this New Road – will in time too become history.

7. LITERARY INFLUENCES

Sir Walter Scott's *Waverley* and *Rob Roy*

Two novels by Sir Walter Scott appear to have exerted a considerable influence on Neil Munro when writing *The New Road*. The first of these is *Waverley* (1814), set at the time of the last major Jacobite Rising of 1745. This is the story of a young Englishman who comes to Scotland as a Captain in the Hanoverian army. He becomes romantically involved with the Jacobite cause, especially in the characters of the chieftain Fergus Mac-Ivor and his beautiful and fanatical sister Flora and eventually Bonnie Prince Charlie himself. After the retreat of the Prince's army from Derby, however, Waverley begins to re-assess the Jacobite cause and the death and suffering it has brought about and decides to abandon it for what he considers to be a more sensible world:

> he felt himself entitled to say firmly, though perhaps with a sigh, that the romance of his

life was ended, and that its real history had
now commenced. (Chapter 60)

But, although he is disillusioned with Jacobitism, he still cares deeply about, and tries to help, his Jacobite friends. Unable to assist Fergus Mac-Ivor he visits him in prison and watches as he marches proudly to his execution.

Like Edward Waverley, at the beginning of *The New Road* Aeneas Macmaster has romantic admiration for the Jacobite Highland chiefs. As he proceeds on his journey northwards, however, he becomes more and more disillusioned by their shabby behaviour until in the end, unlike Edward Waverley, he has complete contempt for them all – except for his father, a Jacobite who had always conducted himself honourably. (See **Theme of Disillusionment** above, p48)

The other Scott novel which seems to have influenced *The New Road* is *Rob Roy* (1818). It is set just before the Jacobite Rising of 1715. Like Edward Waverley its hero, Frank Osbaldistone, is a dreamer but his romanticism is superficial compared with Waverley's. In this novel our interest lies in the attractive and highly practical Glasgow merchant, Bailie Nicol Jarvie. In *The New Road* Munro appears to have drawn on him for his character Alan-Iain-Alain Og, Aeneas's merchant uncle. For Nicol Jarvie, enthusiastic pursuit of trade and commerce is the sensible way forward for a better Scotland, not allegiance to old romantic causes:

> "Now since St Mungo catched herrings in the
> Clyde, what was ever like to gar us flourish
> like the sugar and tobacco trade?" (Chapter
> 26)

Munro's Alan goes much further than the Bailie, however. He wants to use commerce to gain revenge on the Jacobite chiefs whom he blames for having led his brother Paul astray. (See **Theme of Regeneration** above, p53)

Robert Louis Stevenson's *Kidnapped*

Robert Louis Stevenson's great Highland adventure novel *Kidnapped* also seems to have had some influence on *The*

New Road. Central to the plots of both books is the restoration of the rightful heir to his inheritance. Both involve the kidnapping of the young hero, and the fight in the round-house aboard the ship *Covenant* in *Kidnapped* has its equivalent skirmish aboard the *Wayward Lass* in *The New Road*. In both books an evil old man defrauds the young heir of his inheritance. David's Uncle Ebenezer is a vividly portrayed stage villain but he disappears after the first movement of the novel and only reappears at the end to facilitate the restoration of David's fortune. Sandy Duncanson, however, is a much more substantial and complex character. His presence is felt as arch-schemer and double-dealer throughout the book. In addition to defrauding Aeneas of his inheritance we discover him to be a major manipulator of the whole Highland political scene.

It is also true that the young, raw Lowland David Balfour and the charismatic, but sometimes irresponsible, Jacobite Highland Alan Breck have their equivalents in the inexperienced Aeneas Macmaster and mature and reliable Ninian Campbell, but in Munro's novel it must be noted that both of his protagonists are Highlanders – and on the Campbell/Hanoverian side. (See **Theme of Regeneration** above, p53)

8. *THE SEARCH*

The common assumption has been up until now that Munro did not write any more novels after *The New Road* (1914). However, the typescript of eleven chapters of another novel, *The Search*, exists in the National Library of Scotland.[5] It is undated but from Munro's correspondence we can deduce that it was written a few years after *The New Road*. One of the main characters is Ninian Campbell, somewhat older but still *beachdair* and Messenger-at-Arms to the Duke of Argyll. The typescript breaks off in mid-chapter.

The story tells of the arrival of a young horseman in Inveraray called Derry. He is an urbane and sophisticated young man, rather like the hero of Violet Jacob's *Flemington* (1911), and like him he too is a government spy.

The time is about six months after Culloden and his task is to track down a young Jacobite who seems from internal evidence to be called Patrick Drummond and who goes by the alias "Morag".[6]

Derry calls on Sheriff Campbell (clearly modelled on Munro's friend Sheriff John MacMaster Campbell) for further instructions and is introduced to Ninian who is to accompany him in his search for "Morag".

The Jacobite is believed to be in the area of Arisaig, but before heading North Derry is determined to visit the home of the assistant keeper of the prison in Dumbarton. There we are introduced to Colina, an attractive young woman who seems to be the sister of "Morag" although the other characters have no means of knowing this at this point. While they are there a prominent Jacobite, Craigbarnet, escapes from the prison. After this they head for Stirling Castle for further instructions. Receiving none they head North to Doune and Balquhidder. In the meantime Colina dons male clothes and makes for Arisaig to warn "Morag". And there the story stops.

The fragment is well written and the descriptions of Inveraray, Dumbarton and the "top of the town" in Stirling are very evocative. Particularly interesting is the description of Inveraray at the time of the building of the new castle and town, the products of the Enlightenment thinking of the 3rd Duke, Duke Archibald (1743–1761). Again the idea of the need for a more civilised way of life in the Highlands is being dealt with. On the other hand, Ninian with his outlaw Macgregor background, although a man committed to peace, is deeply upset at the thought of the suffering of his fellow Gaels when he sees a herd of a thousand cattle being driven through Doune from Lochaber, the government's compensation to itself for the Jacobite clans' part in the '45, and at the sight of Hanoverian soldiers working the smithy where the Maclaurens had formerly created their famous Doune pistols. The same classic tensions of *The New Road*!

In addition we have the character of Sheriff Campbell who, like Naomi Mitchison's Duncan Forbes of Culloden in her novel *The Bull Calves* (1947), hints that it might be wiser to turn a blind eye and let the Jacobite fugitive go free in contrast to the zealous Derry who would not countenance such an idea.

It is a tantalising fragment dealing again with the Highlands at a crucial period in their history. One can only speculate as to why Munro did not complete it.

Notes

[1] Munro, Neil, *The New Road* (With introduction by Brian D. Osborne), Edinburgh: B & W, 1999: p.ix

[2] Gunn, Neil, *Butcher's Broom*, London: Souvenir Press, 1977: pp72 & 96

[3] John, the 2nd Duke of Argyll (1703–1743), nicknamed "Red John of the Battles". He commanded the government forces against the Jacobites in 1715 and dominated Scottish politics in his later life

[4] Carmichael, Alexander, *Carmina Gadelica*, Vol. 1, No. 20, Edinburgh: Oliver and Boyd, 1928: p53

[5] Munro, Neil, *The Search*, National Library of Scotland MS 26903. Now available in *That Vital Spark: A Neil Munro Anthology* eds. Brian D. Osborne and Ronald Armstrong (Eds.), Edinburgh: Birlinn, 2002

[6] Morag was a code name in Gaeldom which the Jacobites used for their cause, for individual Jacobites and on occasions for Prince Charles Edward Stuart himself

Conclusion

When Neil Munro began writing stories about the Highlands he complained that "all the men who have dealt with the romance of the Highlands hitherto have been Lowlanders, writing from the outside". As a native Gael, familiar with the culture and language of his own people, he believed that he could depict the Highlander authentically and he demonstrates this ability admirably in the portrayal of his main characters in *John Splendid* and *The New Road*. A large part of his success in this is due to his innovative use of language. His sophisticated use of Highland English, which frequently adopts idiomatic Gaelic speech patterns and includes from time to time actual Gaelic words and phrases, helps to create the illusion that the main language of the novels is Gaelic.

The setting of the two novels in the Scottish Highlands is also enhanced by the vivid accuracy with which Munro depicts the mountains and glens and, indeed, the town of Inveraray itself.

Although both novels have strong romantic elements – both have love plots and *The New Road* is of course a murder mystery – they are much more than mere historical romances. Both are written from the Campbell point of view, not from the more popular, sentimental pro-Montrose or pro-Jacobite stance. Both can also claim to fulfil the conditions for Daiches' third category of historical novel (see page 4 above) in that they examine problems which humans have to confront in our own time as well as in earlier centuries: the need to bring peace, progress and prosperity through the rule of law, through trade and through better communications. But to achieve such ends a price sadly will have to be paid and that, in the case of these novels, will be the decline of the old Gaelic way of life – a decline which continues to the present day.

In adopting this approach Neil Munro is following Scott's historical method and it is fitting that the writer R.B. Cunninghame Graham, at the unveiling of Munro's memorial in 1935, called him "the apostolic successor of Sir Walter Scott". Not only, however, is he Scott's successor;

his insightful analysis of the Gael and Highland history opened up a field which would be explored by Scottish novelists of the Highlands of the next and later generations – such writers as Neil Gunn, Naomi Mitchison, Fionn MacColla, Compton MacKenzie and Iain Crichton Smith.

Select Critical Bibliography

Bold, Alan, *Modern Scottish Literature*, London and New York: Longman, 1983.
Burgess, Moira, *Imagine a City: Glasgow in Fiction*, Glendaruel: Argyll Publishing, 1998.
Campbell, Ian, *Kailyard*, Edinburgh: Ramsay Head Press, 1981.
Craig, Cairns (Ed.), *The History of Scottish Literature: Vol. 4 Twentieth Century*: Aberdeen: Aberdeen University press, 1987.
Dickson, Beth, "Foundations of the Modern Scottish Novel" in Craig, 1987 (pp49–60).
Gifford, Douglas (Ed.), *The History of Scottish Literature: Vol. 3 Nineteenth Century*: Aberdeen University Press, 1998.
Gifford, Douglas; Dunnigan, Sarah; MacGillivray, Alan (Eds.), *Scottish Literature*, Edinburgh: Edinburgh University Press, 2002.
Grierson, H.J.C., *Edinburgh Essays on Scots Literature*, Edinburgh: Oliver & Boyd, 1933.
Grieve, Christopher Murray, "Neil Munro", *Contemporary Scottish Studies*, Edinburgh: The Scottish Educational Journal, 1925.
Hart, Francis Russell, *The Scottish Novel: A Critical Survey*, London: John Murray, 1978.
Kohlbek, Beata, *The Fiction and Journalism of Neil Munro: Bridging the Nineteenth and Twentieth Centuries of Scottish Writing*, Unpublished PhD Thesis, University of Glasgow, 2005.
Lendrum, Lesley, *Neil Munro: The Biography*, Colonsay: House of Lochar, 2004.
Lindsay, Maurice, *History of Scottish Literature*, London: Robert Hale, 1977.
MacDiarmid, Hugh, "Neil Munro" in *Contemporary Scottish Studies*, Riach, Alan (Ed.), Manchester: Carcanet, 1995 (pp18–23).
MacDonald, Angus, "Modern Scots Novelists" in Grierson, 1933 (pp144–176).
Mackechnie, Donald, *The Inveraray of Neil Munro*, 1936.
Mackechnie, Donald, *Inveraray Notes*, Oban: The Oban Times, 1986.
Mackechnie, Donald, *Inveraray Tales and Traditions*, 1990.
Power, William, *Literature and Oatmeal: What Literature has Meant to Scotland*, London: George Routledge and Sons, 1935.

Renton, Ronald W., *The Major Fiction of Neil Munro: A Revaluation*, Unpublished M.Phil. Thesis, University of Glasgow, 1997.

Renton, Ronald W. and Osborne, Brian D., *Exploring New Roads: Essays on Neil Munro*, Colonsay: House of Lochar, 2003.

Reid, James, *Modern Scottish Literature*, Edinburgh: Oliver & Boyd, 1945.

Völkel, Hermann, *Das Literarische Werk Neil Munros*, Frankfurt: Peter Lang, 1996.

Watson, Roderick, *The Literature of Scotland*, London: Macmillan, 1984.

Wernitz, Herbert, *Neil Munro und die nationale Kulturbewegung im modernen Schottland*, Berlin: Junker und Dünnhaupt, 1937.

Wittig, Kurt, *The Scottish Tradition in Literature*, Edinburgh: Oliver & Boyd, 1958.

The Works of Neil Munro

SHORT STORY COLLECTIONS

The Lost Pibroch and Other Sheiling Stories, Edinburgh: William Blackwood, 1896.
Ayrshire Idylls (with illustrations by George Houston), London: Adam and Charles Black, 1912.
Jaunty Jock and Other Stories, Edinburgh: William Blackwood, 1918.
The Lost Pibroch, Jaunty Jock, Ayrshire Idylls, Inveraray Edition, Edinburgh: William Blackwood, 1935 (This edition contains the additional story "Ius Primae Noctis" in the *Lost Pibroch* collection.)
The Lost Pibroch and Other Sheiling Stories (with introduction and notes by Ronnie Renton, Rennie McOwan and Rae McGregor), Colonsay: House of Lochar, 1996.
Jaunty Jock and Other Stories (with introduction and notes by Ronnie Renton and Lesley Bratton), Colonsay: House of Lochar, 1999.
Ayrshire Idylls, Edinburgh: FrontList Books (undated).

NOVELS

John Splendid, Edinburgh: William Blackwood, 1898.
Gilian the Dreamer, Edinburgh: William Blackwood, 1899.
Doom Castle, Edinburgh: William Blackwood, 1901.
The Shoes of Fortune, Edinburgh: William Blackwood, 1901.
Children of Tempest, Edinburgh: William Blackwood, 1903.
The Daft Days, Edinburgh: William Blackwood, 1907.
Fancy Farm, Edinburgh: William Blackwood, 1910.
The New Road, Edinburgh: William Blackwood, 1914.
John Splendid (with introduction by Brian D. Osborne), Edinburgh: B & W Publishing, 1994.
Doom Castle (with introduction by Brian D. Osborne), Edinburgh: B & W Publishing, 1996.
The New Road (with introduction by Brian D. Osborne), Edinburgh: B & W Publishing, 1999.
Gilian the Dreamer (with introduction by Douglas Gifford), Edinburgh: B & W Publishing, 2000.
The Daft Days (with introduction by Ronnie Renton), Colonsay: House of Lochar, 2002.
Children of Tempest (with introduction by Ronald Renton), Colonsay: House of Lochar, 2004.

The Shoes of Fortune (with introduction by Ronnie Renton), Gullane: FrontList Books, 2006.

TRAVELOGUE

The Clyde, River and Firth (with illustrations by Mary Y. and J. Young Hunter), London: Adam and Charles Black, 1907.

HUMOROUS SKETCHES

Erchie, My Droll Friend, Edinburgh: William Blackwood, 1904.
The Vital Spark, Edinburgh: William Blackwood, 1906.
In Highland Harbours with Para Handy, Edinburgh: William Blackwood, 1911.
Jimmy Swan, the Joy Traveller, Edinburgh: William Blackwood, 1917.
Hurricane Jack of the Vital Spark, Edinburgh: William Blackwood, 1923.
Para Handy (Complete edition with introduction and notes by Brian D. Osborne and Ronald Armstrong), Edinburgh: Birlinn, 2002.
Erchie, My Droll Friend (Complete edition with introduction and notes by Brian D. Osborne and Ronald Armstrong), Edinburgh: Birlinn, 2002.
Jimmy Swan, The Joy Traveller (with introduction and notes by Brian D. Osborne and Ronald Armstrong), Edinburgh: Birlinn, 2002.

HISTORY

The History of the Royal Bank of Scotland 1727-1927, Edinburgh: (privately printed) 1928.

POETRY

The Poetry of Neil Munro (collected and with preface by John Buchan), Edinburgh: William Blackwood, 1931.

JOURNALISM

The Brave Days (selected and with introduction by George Blake), Edinburgh: The Porpoise Press, 1933.
The Looker On (selected and with introduction by George Blake), Edinburgh: The Porpoise Press, 1933.

ANTHOLOGY

That Vital Spark: A Neil Munro Anthology (edited by Brian D. Osborne and Ronald Armstrong), Edinburgh: Birlinn, 2002 (contains the first ten chapters of *The Search*).